Cheesecakes

Cheesecakes

Maggie Black

Ward Lock Limited · London

FRONT COVER: Black Forest Cheesecake (Picture: Cadbury-Typhoo Food Advisory Service

BACK COVER: Maryland Party Cheesecake with Blackcurrant Purée.

First published in Great Britain in 1980 by Ward Lock Limited, 47 Marylebone Lane, London W1M 6AX, a Pentos Company.

Designed by Chris Walker
House editor Frances Dixon
Text filmset in Korinna Regular by Facet Filmsetting Limited, Southend-on-Sea, Essex

Printed and bound in Singapore by Toppan Printing Company

British Library Cataloguing in Publication Data

Black, Maggie
  Cheesecakes.
  1. Cheesecake (Cookery)
  I. Title
  641.6'7'3   TX773

ISBN 0 7063 5853 8

Contents

Introduction   7

Cheeses and curds to use   8

Baking and chilling cheesecakes   10

Making soft cheeses   11

Other main ingredients   12

Pastry, batters and sponges   13

Crumb crusts and coatings   15

Baked cheesecakes   17

Gelatine-set cheesecakes   46

Other unbaked cheesecakes and flans   68

Low-cost cheesecakes   75

Small cheesecakes   81

Toppings and sauces   91

Index   95

Acknowledgements

The publisher and author would like to thank the following for their co-operation and assistance in the production of this book.

For recipes:
Bird's Desserts
Cadbury-Typhoo Food Advisory Service
Dairy Produce Advisory Service of the Milk Marketing Board
English Country Cheese Council
Farmhouse English Cheese Information Office
Judy Ridgway
Kaserei Champignon, West Germany
Kellogg Company of Great Britain Ltd.
Longley Farm, Holmfirth, Yorkshire
Luxembourg Tourist Office
Swiss Cheese Union
Unigate Foods (St. Ivel) Ltd.
United Rum Merchants Ltd.

For test materials:
Billingtons Natural Brown Sugars
Farm House Bakery Products Ltd. (Hopper's)
Farmhouse English Cheese Information Office
Gate Delicatessen Ltd., London N6
Golden Wonder Potato Crisps
Lesmé Ltd.
Longley Farm (for all cottage cheese used)
Swiss Cheese Union
United Rum Merchants Ltd.
Weight Watchers International Inc.

For cover picture:
Cadbury-Typhoo Food Advisory Service

The pictures on the back cover and pages 24, 29, 32 and 36 were taken by Edmund Goldspink; those on pages 25, 28, 33, 37, 45, 48, 49, 56, 60, 64, 65, 72 and 84 were taken by Louis Jordaan.

NOTES
It is important to follow **either** the metric **or** the imperial measures when using these recipes.
All spoon measures are level.
Flour is plain and sugar is granulated unless otherwise specified.

Introduction

Cheesecakes are not a modern invention. They may well have been the first desserts ever made. The ancient Egyptians and Sumerians ate them. So did biblical, migrant tribes, following their flocks. In ancient Greece, wedding cakes were cheesecakes.

Those early cheesecakes were created and eaten in warm climates where fresh milk and cream soured quickly, but where grass, and therefore milk-giving animals, were common. All round the Mediterranean, from the steppe lands of south Russia and the Balkans to the Middle East, desserts made with soft cheeses are still one of the most practical ways to use the food value of whole milk; certainly for the peasant farmers, who still make their own curd cheeses as a matter of habit. A goatskin bag of soft cheese hangs outside every second cottage in any small Greek or Israeli village, and every household tent of a pastoral Arab tribe.

The cheesecakes these people make, now traditional favourite foods all over eastern Europe, are often rich, solid mixtures, made with full-fat soft cheese and cultured or soured cream; they often contain dried fruit, and are given a baked-on soured cream topping. They are usually only 5–8 cm (2–3 inches) deep, and are baked in a pastry or crumb shell, so they often look more like tarts or flans. Being convenient to transport, they became characteristically Jewish foods many centuries ago, and are now familiar, well-loved desserts wherever Jewish communities have found a home.

In western Europe, especially England, a different tradition developed. In medieval days, in the dairy of any wealthy man's castle or manor, the rich milk from cows on lush pasture was often allowed to stand until the cream could be skimmed off to use for butter-making. The best of the slightly soured milk was then set as soft cheese for the lord of the manor and his lady to eat as 'white meats', especially on the many fast days imposed by the early Church. These wealthy aristocrats loved sweet foods, so cheesecakes were among the most popular 'white meats' they enjoyed. Their cheesecakes were often set with plenty of well-whisked eggs, making up for the forbidden meat.

Another kind of cheesecake made with eggs was developed in traditional English cookery too. Our word cheese once just meant curds, the semi-pasty clots of milk solids made by souring milk naturally or setting it with an acid such as rennet. Very early, dairymaids and cooks noticed that eggs, finely ground rice or beans, and some other foods, made the same kind of soft, semi-clotted paste, when warmed with milk as milk curds set with rennet. So these products and others like them came to be called cheeses—thick custards, ground rice or nut gruels, and even mixtures of long-simmered fruit which contained no milk at all.

English cookery already contained a wealth of recipes for small custard and similar tartlets eaten as festival snacks at the big parish fairs held on saints' days. These little feast-day custard cakes, often named after particular saints, naturally came to be called cheesecakes. Traditional regional cookery still contains dozens of them, as well as versions of the old egg curd preserve still called lemon cheese by older people, although lemon curd is its modern name.

These custard-style cheesecakes remained popular for centuries. They were the kind which the Puritans took with them to America in Stuart times. There, the emigrants met other sectarians from eastern Europe with their more solid, richer cheesecakes. The mixture of traditions led, in time, to the development of a new, typical all-American cheesecake. This is the type we generally picture when we think of a cheesecake. It is usually set on a pastry or crumb base instead of in a shell, and is up to 10 cm (4 inches) deep. The mixture is generally based on full-fat soft cheese with cream added, and is lightened with whisked eggs. It may be baked but is quite likely to be set with gelatine instead. Toppings vary widely, but are nearly always colourful; jam glaze or sliced fruit are the most popular.

Some American party cheesecakes consist just of the set cheese mixture coated with crumbs. These tortes, as they are sometimes called, are served as a rich dessert with whipped cream. Like other American cheesecakes, they will often serve 12–16 people. Most American cheesecakes, for all their fragile fluffiness, are richer than they seem; their curd and egg-white lightness is deceptive.

Most of the recipes in this book are for traditional, rich cheesecakes, tarts and flans, and the fluffier American cheesecakes in all their variety. They range from rich, luxurious party cheesecakes to low-fat and economical ones. There is also a section of recipes for small cheesecakes and tartlets, some made from cheeses and some from custard mixtures. They have lots of practical uses, as snacks at coffee time or with afternoon tea, and they have good protein value for packed meals. You will find them just as useful, in their own way, as the large, traditional festival cheesecakes and the cream-based American cheesecakes which are now among our most popular desserts.

Cheeses and curds to use

Most cheesecakes are made with soft cheese. All soft cheeses consist of partly-drained milk curds made from milk soured naturally or set with rennet or other acid. They may be made from whole full-fat milk, skimmed milk, or may have cream or butter added to make a richer cheese. They may be heat-treated, as cottage cheese is, to set the curd more firmly. Most soft cheeses are salted to preserve them for a short time and to give them a more interesting flavour.

Simple soft cheeses were first made in home kitchens, to use milk which would otherwise go bad rather than sour. Milk which is going bad tastes bitter instead of having the pleasant sharpness of sour milk. To prevent milk going bad, housewives from early times onward usually set the milk curds themselves rather than wait for them to sour naturally. Some made cultured milks such as yogurt; others used rennet or acid from herbs to set the milk. The set, thickened milk was then hung in a cloth or skin bag to drain off most of the liquid or whey containing the milk sugars (the part of the milk which goes bad). The curd was forked over and scraped down from time to time, until it was as dense or stiff as the housewife wanted. Then she added salt, and perhaps butter or cream if the household could afford it, and shaped her cheese into a pat or put it in a mould.

If the milk had been allowed to stand, to skim off the cream, it might already be turning sour. In this case, it was simply put near the fire or on the side of the stove to let the gentle heat separate the curds or 'clabber' and whey before they could go bad. The cheese was then hung up to drip in the usual way.

Housewives in all dairying areas of the world still make these soft cheeses in their own kitchens. The cheeses differ with the kind of milk used and its richness, and they have different names in different countries. Pot cheese, farmer's cheese, clabber cheese, curd cheese, junket cheese, and yogurt cheese are names used in the English-speaking world. The French FROMAGE BLANC, German QUARK-KASE, Italian RICOTTA and Greek MYZITHRA are all versions of the same simple, semi-drained type of cheese, although they are lighter and sharper-flavoured than most English and American ones.

You can use home-made cheese or any of these bought cheeses for making cheesecakes provided they have the right quantity of butterfat for the recipe.

In Britain soft cheeses are divided into six grades, depending on how much butterfat they have, and the Trade Descriptions Act has laid down what each grade of cheese must be called. The grades are:

less than 2% butterfat	skimmed milk soft cheese
2–10% butterfat	low-fat soft cheese
10–20% butterfat	medium-fat soft cheese
20–45% butterfat	full-fat soft cheese
45–65% butterfat	*cream cheese
over 65% butterfat	*double cream cheese

The names low-fat, medium-fat and so on are now printed on the packets or cartons of most soft cheeses, foreign as well as British, so you can swap one brand for another of the same grade if you like its

*Cream cheeses are seldom true cheeses; usually they are not made from curds, just drained, set cream.

flavour or texture better. Go by the grade names (low-fat etc.) not the butterfat percentages, which are calculated in different ways in different countries.

One other point about soft cheeses may be confusing; many of the richer, full-fat soft cheeses are what we used to call cream cheeses, and quite a number of retailers still sell them as such. Do not be misled. If you are offered cream cheese, say in a delicatessen, ask to see the label on the manufacturer's carton; the chances are that it will have 'Full-Fat Soft Cheese' written on it. Real cream cheese is rarely sold because it is too rich for most people's taste, it is expensive, and it goes off very quickly.

A few recipes for traditional cheesecakes call for the use of unsalted soft cheese. For these recipes you can sometimes get unsalted soft cheese in a health food store. An easier alternative may be to make your own so a recipe for home-made cheese which is firm, and therefore suitable, is given on page 11.

Whether you buy or make the soft cheese, it will not keep long, once made. Although soft cheeses were invented as a way of preserving milk, they are a very short-term preserve. Your cheese will get progressively sharper-flavoured every day, so use it quickly. Cheesecakes were first developed as one way of preserving soft cheese just a little longer, and in fact one of the great merits of many cheesecakes is that they can, and should, be kept for 1–2 days or even longer before use. Many cheesecakes also freeze perfectly which most soft cheeses do not; unless they are very rich in fat they go grainy.

Their keeping quality makes cheesecakes especially convenient as party desserts because you can make them ahead of time. Another good feature is that they are so adaptable; a modern cheesecake can be as rich or plain as you wish. It can also, provided the cheese is still fairly bland, be given almost any flavouring you like.

Baking and chilling cheesecakes

Baked cheesecakes often behave like soufflés. They rise dramatically while being baked, then sink ignominiously when taken out of the oven. After two or three such experiences, it is tempting to leave a cheesecake in the oven for 5–10 minutes longer than the stated time, to set it more firmly. This is usually a mistake; the cheesecake still falls, and is tough through over-baking. It is better to underbake a cheesecake slightly, i.e. to turn off the oven heat when it is only just set. Even more important, almost any cheesecake should be cooled very slowly. As a general rule, never take a cheesecake out of a hot oven into a cold draughty atmosphere, dump it on a cold surface or remove the tin while it is still hot and let cold air circulate round it. Many recipes for baked cheesecakes in this book direct you to cool the cheesecake in the turned-off oven with the door ajar. Always, in fact, do this unless some other specific direction is given. Even if the cheesecake does still sink—and most do—it will be less dense in texture and will crack less than if cooled suddenly.

Many cheesecakes crack as they cool. Do not worry about this. They may look less glamorous, but their flavour is not affected. For party use, a fruit topping or rosettes of cream will cover the cracks.

A cheesecake baked or chilled for the correct time to set it lightly may still seem wobbly or moist if the tin or mould is then removed at once. Again, one may be tempted to bake it longer or blame the recipe for not including enough gelatine. The mistake, however, is in removing the tin or mould too soon. Almost all cheesecakes firm up considerably during the 24 hours after being made, and as a general rule, all cheesecakes should be kept for 24 hours in the refrigerator or a cold larder before being served. In this book, special directions to serve at once are given for any cheesecake which should be served as soon as it is made. All other cheesecakes should be kept for several hours at least before being served. If a longer storage period is needed, the recipe says so.

Freezing cheesecakes

Plain baked cheesecakes freeze perfectly. Gelatine-set cheesecakes can be frozen unless they contain custard or a high proportion of whole eggs or fresh fruit. If they contain any of these, they will break down when thawed. Clear jelly toppings will go cloudy in storage.

Cheesecakes which are, in fact, custard flans, tarts or tartlets should not be frozen.

Other cheesecakes should be frozen without a topping or decorations. Most nut, crumb, jam and fruit toppings can be frozen separately. Sauces to accompany the cheesecakes can also be frozen separately. Rich double cream can be frozen, whipped or unwhipped, but whipping and single cream will go grainy in storage.

Cheesecakes should be frozen without wrappings, then wrapped for storage. They should be unwrapped before thawing to avoid any risk of damaging the soft, thawed cheesecake. Baked cheesecakes generally take 3–4 hours to thaw at room temperature, unbaked cheesecakes 2–3 hours, depending on their size and contents.

Making soft cheeses

Cheese is made by minute bacteria called STREP-TOCOCCUS LACTIS or 'STREP LACTIS'. (Yogurt is made by similar bacteria.) STREP LACTIS occurs naturally in raw milk, but there are no bacteria in pasteurized milk; so they must be put back to make the milk sour and set instead of go putrid.

Most people wait for the milk to go sour naturally, with the help of STREP LACTIS from the air, but it may be risky. A surer way is to put a culture or starter of the right bacteria into the milk. The easiest way to do it is to add a rennet tablet or some yogurt to the milk, and make junket or yogurt cheese.

Home-Made Milk Curd Cheese
Makes about 125 g (4 oz) cheese

600 ml (1 pint) whole or skimmed milk
rennet essence or unflavoured rennet
   tablet to set 600 ml (1 pint) milk
$\frac{1}{4}$–$\frac{1}{2}$ teaspoon salt (optional)

Make a firm unsweetened junket with the milk and rennet as directed on the rennet bottle. Scald a thin square cloth or man's handkerchief. Lay it over a sieve balanced on a basin, with the corners hanging loose. Tip in the junket. Gather up the corners of the cloth, tie them together to form a bag, and hang it up to drain. After 6–8 hours, scrape down any curd on the sides of the cloth into the main mass, turn the curd over, and rehang the bag. Repeat this process after another 6–8 hours if the cheese is still wetter than you want it. When the cheese has the texture you want, add salt to taste for savoury use if desired; use very little salt for cheesecakes. Work the salt into the cheese, then pack the cheese in a carton, cover and refrigerate. Alternatively, form into a pat for immediate use. Use as a low-fat soft cheese.

NOTE: cream can be added to the cheese if a richer (full-fat) cheese is wanted.

Yogurt Cheese
Makes about 125 g (4 oz) cheese

600–750 ml (1–1$\frac{1}{4}$ pints) natural yogurt
salt (optional)

Drain the yogurt in the same way as junket (see previous recipe). When it has the texture you want, work in a little salt if desired, turn the cheese into a carton, and refrigerate for not more than 48 hours before use. Yogurt makes a firm, smooth cheese particularly suitable for cheesecakes. Use as a low-fat soft cheese.

Lemon Cheese Filling
(an old Essex recipe)
Makes about 600 ml (1 pint) filling to store

175 g (6 oz) butter
250 g (8 oz) icing sugar
60 g (2 oz) ground rice
grated rind and juice 1 lemon
2 eggs

Soften the butter and sift the icing sugar. Beat the butter until very soft and creamy. Beat or work in the icing sugar gradually, then blend in the ground rice and lemon rind until smooth. Separately, beat the eggs and lemon juice until blended, then mix thoroughly with the butter-sugar mixture. Beat well for 2–3 minutes. Turn the mixture into a scalded pot, dried in the oven and cooled. Seal with a screw-top or similar lid, and refrigerate until required. The mixture will keep for 2–4 weeks.

To use, half-fill shortcrust or puff pastry cases, baked blind for 7–8 minutes. Bake at 200°C, 400°F, Gas 6, for 12–14 minutes for shallow cases, 20–30 minutes for deep ones, until risen and golden. Cool in the turned-off oven with the door ajar.

Other main ingredients

Certain ingredients besides cheese feature regularly in cheesecakes old and new.

All baked cheesecakes and some others contain EGGS. Size 4 or 5 eggs have been used in making these recipes.

Many unbaked cheesecakes are set with GELATINE. Sometimes it is in the form of a flavoured jelly tablet which will set 600 ml (1 pint) liquid. Usually, however, it is unflavoured granulated (powdered) gelatine which is sold in packets holding 15 g ($\frac{1}{2}$ oz), which is 1 tablespoon.

CREAM is used in a lot of cheesecakes. It may be double cream containing at least 48% butterfat, whipping cream with at least 35% butterfat, which makes lighter cheesecakes, or single cream with a minimum of 18% butterfat. Quite a lot of recipes use soured cream (18% butterfat) because, originally, one function of cheesecakes was to preserve cream which had already soured and would soon go bad.

All the recipes in this book use standard quality cream, normally sold in waxed cartons holding 142 ml (5 fl oz) and 284 ml (10 fl oz) in Britain. U.H.T. (ultra heat treated) cream, which keeps for months on the shelf in its sealed waxed carton, is just as suitable as ordinary short-lived pasteurized cream. Whipping cream is particularly useful to keep in this form. Its 35–42% butterfat makes it a better consistency for whipping than double cream, and the heat treatment does not destroy the flavour of the fresh cream. Sterilized creams which are longer-lived have an altered flavour.

Eastern European and Balkan cheesecakes, and some modern American ones, are often made with natural (unflavoured) YOGURT instead of soured cream. Almost all the yogurt sold commercially today is low-fat yogurt made from skimmed milk, and so the recipes in this book have been adapted to use it. One or two recipes in the book use the popular, new fruit-flavoured yogurts; the ingredients list tells you which to use in each case.

A point to notice about the yogurt in all these recipes is that it is treated as a liquid; the quantity to use is given in millilitres, and in fractions of a pint or fluid ounces. Some, although not all, commercial yogurt is sold by weight, in grams or ounces. So it is always wise to measure the yogurt in a measuring jug before using it. Stir it gently to liquify it before measuring.

Another point to watch is the sell-by date on the carton. Fresh yogurt should always be used for cheesecakes if possible. Any yogurt gets more acid day by day and may be too acid for a cheesecake by the end of its shelf life.

Most cheesecakes have at least a hint of LEMON flavouring to give them a tang. As a rule, the cheese's flavour should dictate just how much lemon tang it needs, so most recipes simply tell you to use the juice and/or rind of $\frac{1}{2}$ or 1 lemon; the size of lemon is left to you. As a guide, however, the recipes throughout this book have used whole lemons weighing 90 g (3 oz) each.

For cheesecakes which contain only lemon juice, without rind, unsweetened bottled or canned lemon juice can be used instead of fresh juice. Use 2 tablespoons of juice instead of each whole lemon. As a rule, bottled or canned juice does not need straining. Fresh juice should only be strained if you want a very smooth cheesecake filling; otherwise, the minute fragments of lemon flesh give it an interesting texture.

As for the rind, grate off just the thin yellow outer skin whch contains the flavouring oil or zest. The white pith underneath is bitter. In one or two recipes its extra roughness is needed; then the recipe specifies that the whole peel (rind and pith) should be used. Always use freshly-grated rind.

Many traditional cheesecakes contain DRIED FRUIT as well as lemon. Raisins or sultanas, once called golden raisins, are the most usual dried fruit in these cheesecakes. Stoned and seedless raisins are both widely available in packets, ready washed and dried. Stoned raisins are larger and juicier but they may be too heavy in a light cheesecake, so they are best kept for the creamier, denser fillings. Seedless raisins, which are smaller and cheaper, do just as well if you soak them in boiling water for a short time. However it is most important to pat them dry thoroughly before using them; wet raisins in a cheesecake are disastrous.

Modern dessert cheesecakes have many other fruit flavourings, using WHOLE FRUIT or only juice. Whole fruit may be fresh, frozen or canned. It may be used sliced under the filling mixture or placed on top; or it may be made into an almost set purée or glaze. Fresh fruit almost always has a more vital flavour, but canned fruit is more vivid and is available all year round. Make sure that all fruit is really well drained; if not it will make a soggy mess of the cheesecake filling or crust under it. Fresh fruit in cheesecakes usually has sugar added. Canned fruit may be in its own juice or in syrup, and either may be added to the cheesecake mixture for extra flavour.

Some cheesecakes are almost unsweetened; others are very sweet, especially if made with fruit syrup. Cheesecakes are normally sweetened with white SUGAR. Brown sugar makes then dingy instead of deliciously snowy-white or lemon-gold, and the flavour of the brown sugar may mask the clean, fresh taste of the cheese and lemon. However, you can use a light muscovado or similar brown sugar for any cheesecake if you wish. Honey, although deliciously flavoured, may be hazardous to use unless a recipe is designed for it; it changes the consistency of the mixture, and may give it a sticky texture if used in any quantity.

Cheesecakes may have many other ingredients to give them firmness, colour or flavour. Originally, wholemeal, rye or potato flour was used for traditional cheesecakes, but today WHITE FLOUR is almost always used for both pastry crusts and fillings, for lightness. SPICES and NUTS give flavour and texture to the older, more solid cheesecakes. The more delicate, fluffier modern ones may have a LIQUEUR teamed with fruit to make them luxury desserts.

Pastry, batters and sponges

Many cheesecakes, especially the traditional rich ones from eastern Europe, are baked in a pastry case or shell. Any standard pastry suitable for sweet dishes may be used except flaky and choux pastry. Large or heavy cheesecakes need a solid casing which will not crack when removed from the baking tin. This is one reason why many traditional cheesecakes have a rich, shortcrust pastry shell. Rich pastry is also much less likely to toughen during the long cooking time that is required by a large cheesecake.

If the cheesecake filling has a distinct flavour besides that of the sweetened cheese, the pastry for its case is often flavoured to suit it. For instance, ground cinnamon or ginger may be added to the pastry flour if the filling is spicy or fruit-flavoured, or ground almonds may replace some of the flour for an almond-flavoured cheesecake.

Any pastry case, flavoured or not, may be filled while still uncooked and be baked with its filling, or it may be baked blind (see page 14) before being filled. It depends on the type of filling, how moist it is, and for how long and at what temperature it will be baked, if at all. You will find flat, flan-style cheese-cakes with both types of case in this book. A large cheesecake baked in a deep cake tin seldom has a pastry case, but when it does, the bottom of the case is usually baked blind first, and the uncooked sides are fitted into the tin and sealed to the baked pastry just before the filling mixture is put in.

Small curd (custard) cheesecakes or tartlets are baked in uncooked or pre-baked cases exactly like large, flan-style cheesecakes.

Every pastry-cased cheesecake recipe in this book either includes the recipe for its own special pastry, or suggests the quantity and type of standard pastry to use. In each case, the pastry has been carefully chosen to suit the texture or flavour of the cheesecake. Moist or heavy fillings, especially fruit-filled ones, should always be baked in the recom-mended pastry. For lighter cheesecakes you can use your own favourite pastry, or bought frozen pastry for convenience. To make it easy, recipes using stan-dard pastry give the quantity as ready-made dough.

Some pastry mixtures for casing cheesecakes are so rich or soft that they cannot be rolled out easily. This type of mixture is sometimes called a pressed pastry. A pressed pastry dough is, literally, pressed in an even layer on to the base and sides of a greased baking tin or flan case, like a crumb crust. This is usually done most easily with the back of a spoon, although an even richer, moister mixture may need to be spread with a knife. Some spreading mixtures which contain only a little flour are more like batter than pastry.

Occasionally, a cheesecake has a real batter base, which is poured into the tin, and baked before the cheesecake mixture is put on top.

For a lighter foundation, a Genoese or similar sponge base is sometimes used instead of pastry. A sponge base is always baked and cooled before the cheesecake mixture is put on top. It makes a delicate yet firm base for a fluffy party cheesecake.

A lot of modern cheesecakes have a crumb crust base or casing, or they may have no base at all, only a light coating of crumbs. These are almost all dessert cheesecakes.

Rich Shortcrust or Flan Pastry
Makes 250 g (8 oz) pastry

125 g (4 oz) flour
salt
40 g (1½ oz) margarine
40 g (1½ oz) lard
1 teaspoon castor sugar
1 egg
cold water as required

Sift the flour and a pinch of salt together. Rub in the fats with the fingertips, until the mixture resembles fine breadcrumbs. Mix in the sugar. Blend the egg with a few drops of water, and use to bind the mix-ture. Knead lightly until the dough is smooth and without cracks. Allow to stand for 10 minutes. Roll out, without stretching, on a lightly floured board. Use at once, or fold, wrap in clingfilm, and chill for up to 24 hours before use. Bake, as a rule, at 200°C, 400°F, Gas 6.

To Line and Bake a Pastry Case Blind
Grease the inside of a sandwich cake tin, flan case or flan ring set on a heavy baking sheet. Roll out the pastry on a lightly floured board. Lift it on the rolling pin, and lay it on the tin. Lift the edges of the pastry, and lower the centre portion on to the base of the tin. Ease the pastry into the tin to cover the whole base. Press it lightly into the angle between the base and sides, and up the sides. Cut off any excess pastry at the top edge of the tin, or make a decorative fluted edge around the top. Prick the base of the pastry lightly with a fork. Cut out a circle of greaseproof paper slightly larger than the tin, grease it lightly and fit it into the tin, greased side down. Fill it with dried beans or rice. Bake for 10–15 minutes at 190°C, 375°F, Gas 5, or at the main recipe temperature, until it is firm and just beginning to brown at the top. Remove the beans or rice and the paper, and return to the oven for 5 minutes to dry out the base of the case. Cool if necessary and use as required, or store for up to 48 hours in an airtight tin before use.

To Bake a Pastry Base for a Deep Cake Tin

You will need nearly twice as much pastry as for a flan ring of the same diameter; the exact quantity will depend on the depth of the tin.

Roll out the pastry on a lightly floured board, and cut out a round which will fit the base of the tin. Cut out separately a strip or strips which will fit the sides of the tin. Keep these strips aside. Turn the tin upside down, and grease the underside of the base lightly.

Lay the pastry round on it. Put in the oven and bake at the main recipe temperature until the pastry is firm but not yet browned. Cool. Remove the pastry, and turn the tin right way up. Lightly grease the inside of the tin. Lay the baked pastry round in the base, and dampen the edges with water. Fit the uncooked pastry strips round the sides, sealing them to the baked base with light pressure. Fill with the chosen filling, and bake as the recipe requires.

Crumb crusts and coatings

Modern cheesecakes more often have a crumb crust than a pastry shell or base. The crust is not a top covering, but a crusty layer or shell made of ready-baked fine bread, biscuit or cake crumbs mixed with fat and with sugar (for plain crumbs). It supports the cheesecake exactly like a pastry base.

As a rule plain or sweet biscuit crumbs are used to make crumb crusts for cheesecakes, although you will find one or two breadcrumb and cake crumb bases suggested in this book, and even bases made of breakfast food flakes, potato crisps, sliced cake or trifle sponges. Biscuit crumbs are the most convenient to use because they can be stored in an airtight jar or tin on the shelf for weeks before going musty. They are also a good way to use up broken biscuits or the last few biscuits in a packet, by mixing them with other, similar biscuit crumbs.

Digestive biscuit crumbs are most often used for their semi-sweet, slightly nutty flavour, but there are many other interesting kinds as illustrated in the table on page 16.

Consider the flavour and texture of your cheesecake or topping before deciding what type of crumbs to use. Sharp-flavoured fruit cheesecakes, such as redcurrant or apricot ones, usually need a smooth crust of plain biscuit crumbs made with Marie or similar biscuits. Classic lemon cheesecakes, however, welcome the contrasting texture of digestive or gingernut crumbs. A spicy cheesecake will take the more insistent flavour of crispbreads or oatcakes, while a fragile, luxurious party cheesecake is best on a smooth, sweet crust. Every crumb-based cheesecake recipe in this book suggests a type of crumb that is suitable, but you may use another type if you prefer.

Crumbs are all made in the same way. Break up biscuits, crispbreads or cookies roughly. Put the pieces between two sheets of stout paper; the top sheet is needed to prevent the crumbs scattering. Roll a heavy rolling pin or bottle over the top sheet of paper. Remove any rice paper from macaroon crumbs, and any hard or lumpy bits from other biscuits, and roll again until the crumbs are fine and even. Tip them into a jar with an airtight lid, and store on the shelf or in the refrigerator, until they are required for use.

Biscuits to Use for Crumb Crusts

Type of biscuit	Crumbs
water biscuits, cream crackers	smooth, unflavoured, unsweetened, dry
wheat crispbreads, rusks	slightly grainy, nutty-flavoured, unsweetened, dry
oatcakes (plain or sweetened), bran biscuits, some crispbreads	grainy, nutty-flavoured, unsweetened or semi-sweet, dry
plain biscuits such as Marie, Butter Osborne, Rich Tea and most breakfast food flakes	smooth, slightly sweetened, dry
sweet biscuits such as Lincoln, Petit Beurre	smooth, sweet, no marked flavour, dry
sweet flavoured biscuits such as gingernuts, spice biscuits	smooth, sweet, marked flavour, dry
shortbreads, digestive biscuits, chocolate biscuits, chocolate digestive biscuits (plain or milk), oatmeal parkin	smooth or slightly grainy, semi-sweet or sweet, flavoured, rich
macaroons, peanut and other nut biscuits	grainy or fibrous, full-flavoured, rich

Any crumb crust is bound with softened or melted fat. Almost always, butter, margarine or melted chocolate is used, depending on the flavour of the cheesecake and crumbs; hard margarine or soft tub margarine is equally suitable.

As a rule, unflavoured, dry and slightly sweetened crumbs have sweetening added. The commonest sweetening is sugar but you can use honey, jam, golden syrup, treacle or molasses if you wish. Take care not to make the mixture sticky or it may 'weep' later, and will stick to the tin and be messy to cut when served.

A variety of interesting crusts may be made by adding flavouring, or ingredients which change the crust's texture. Try ground cinnamon or mace, allspice, mixed spice or grated nutmeg for a spiced crust. Add crushed wheat, grated or finely chopped nuts, desiccated or toasted coconut, sesame seeds or soaked poppy seeds for texture interest.

All crumb crusts are made in the same way. The crumbs are mixed with any other dry ingredients, and the fat is worked in with a fork or the back of a spoon, to make a crumbly or a pasty mixture. A liquid sweetening is usually worked in with the fat. The mixture is then pressed or spread over the base, or the base and sides, of the cake tin, flan case, flan ring or pie plate in which the cheesecake is to be baked or chilled. A cake tin should have a removable base, and any container should be well greased inside, or, better still, be lined with greased paper before putting in the crumb mixture. The crust is then chilled to firm it up, or it may be baked for 8–10 minutes to crisp it. A moist cheesecake is best on a pre-baked crust to avoid any risk of it being soggy.

When you line a flan case or ring completely with a crumb crust, make the sides the same thickness all the way up; when pressing the mixture into place, one can easily make the sides too thin and fragile at the top so that they crumble. When the case is complete, slice off any bits of crust which stick up, using a sharp knife held horizontally. Then brush off any loose crumbs on the top and inside of the case.

However, if you make a base and a shallow 2.5 cm (1 inch) rim to support a higher cheesecake mixture, make the top edge as thin as you can, to avoid biting into a doorstep of crust near the base of the cheesecake.

Some dessert cheesecakes, especially party ones, do not have a solid base at all. Instead, they have a thin coating of crumbs sprinkled all over the inside of a well-greased container before the filling mixture is put in. Only 30–40 g (1–1½ oz) of crumbs are needed, even for a big cake tin.

Another, and decorative, way to use crumbs on a cheesecake is to press them gently with your palms on to the sides of an unbaked cheesecake after removing the container. The pressure must be gentle and the crumbs fairly fine since some of these cheesecakes are fragile. Finely chopped or ground nuts, or desiccated coconut can also be used in the same way.

Baked cheesecakes

Cottage Cheese Torte
Serves 6

Base and Topping
40 g (1½ oz) any sweet biscuit crumbs
Filling
2×226 g (8 oz) cartons cottage cheese
60 g (2 oz) butter
2 eggs
2 tablespoons double cream
125 g (4 oz) castor sugar
grated rind and juice 1 lemon
salt
60 g (2 oz) flour

Line the base and, using butter, grease the inside of a 20 cm (8 inch) loose-based cake tin. Dust the inside of the tin with 30 g (1 oz) of the crumbs. Put the remaining crumbs aside. Sieve the cheese into a bowl. Melt the butter over gentle heat, add to the cheese and beat them together. Then beat in the eggs one at a time. When well blended, lightly beat in the cream, sugar, lemon rind and juice, a pinch of salt and the flour. Pour into the tin and scatter the reserved crumbs on top. Bake at 180°C, 350°F, Gas 4, for 45 minutes or until firm and browned. Cool in the tin. Run a sharp knife round the sides of the tin to loosen the cooled cheesecake, and remove from the tin. Refrigerate for at least 4 hours before serving.

Snowy Party Cheesecake
Serves 8–10

Base
30 g (1 oz) gingernut crumbs
Filling
3×227 g (8 oz) packets Philadelphia soft cheese
1 teaspoon vanilla essence
4 egg whites
150 g (5 oz) castor sugar
Topping
pineapple topping (see page 92)

Generously grease the inside of a 20 cm (8 inch) springform cake tin. Sprinkle the crumbs over the base and sides pressing them on firmly. To make the filling, bring the cheese up to room temperature. Cream the cheese and vanilla essence together until soft. Separately, whisk the egg whites until foamy, then whisk in the sugar gradually, beating well after each addition. Continue whisking until the whites are stiff and glossy. Fold them into the cheese mixture. Turn gently into the cake tin. Bake at 180°C, 350°F, Gas 4, for 25 minutes. The centre will still be soft. Cool slowly, in the turned-off oven with the door ajar. Then refrigerate for at least 4 hours before removing from the tin. Top with the pineapple topping (see page 92) just before serving.

This cheesecake is very white, light and moist. Cut it with a thin, sharp paring knife.

Adaptable Cheesecake

Serves 8

Base and Topping
100 g (3½ oz) butter or margarine
250 g (8 oz) digestive biscuit or
    sweet oatcake crumbs
60 g (2 oz) castor sugar
1½ teaspoons ground cinnamon

Filling
3 eggs, separated
125 g (4 oz) castor sugar
350 g (12 oz) full-fat and low-fat
    soft cheeses, mixed (see note below)
grated rind and juice 1 lemon
150 ml (¼ pint) single, double or soured
    cream, or a mixture

Line the base and grease the inside of a 20 cm (8 inch) loose-based cake tin. Melt the fat without letting it get too hot. Put the crumbs in a bowl. Add the fat and mix until the crumbs will stick together when pressed. Separately, mix together the sugar and cinnamon. Put 2 tablespoons aside, and combine the rest with the fat-covered crumbs. Press the crumb mixture evenly over the base and sides of the tin. Chill while making the filling.

Mix the egg yolks and sugar, and beat until thick and creamy. Sieve the cheeses together, using the proportions you prefer or find convenient. Mix the sieved cheeses lightly into the egg-sugar mixture. Then lightly mix in the lemon rind and juice, and the cream. Whisk the egg whites to the same consistency as the cheese mixture. Stir in 2 tablespoons, then fold in the rest. Turn the mixture gently into the chilled shell. Bake at 170°C, 325°F, Gas 3, for 45–50 minutes. Sprinkle with the reserved sugar and cinnamon, and bake 15 minutes longer. Cool in the tin. Run a sharp knife round the inside of the tin to loosen the cheesecake, and turn out for serving.

NOTE: the higher the proportion of full-fat cheese, the richer the cheesecake will be. 125 g (4 oz) full-fat cheese with 250 g (8 oz) low-fat cheese will give a cheesecake of average richness if you use double cream. Single cream will give you a lighter cheesecake; soured cream a tangier one.

Saffron Cheesecake

Serves 8

Base
250 g (8 oz) self-raising flour
salt
125 g (4 oz) white fat (Spry or Trex)
4–5 tablespoons cold water

Filling
saffron strands or powder
2 teaspoons boiling water
125 g (4 oz) castor sugar
3 eggs, separated
350 g (12 oz) low-fat soft cheese
30 g (1 oz) butter
1 tablespoon lemon juice
100 ml (4 fl oz) soured cream
salt

Using butter, grease the inside of a 23 cm (9 inch) flan ring on a baking sheet. Sift the flour and salt into a bowl. Rub in the fat with the fingertips, and mix to a dough with the water. Knead lightly, then chill for 30 minutes. Roll out the pastry on a lightly floured board, and use it to line the ring. Bake blind (see page 14), and cool.

To make the filling infuse a good pinch of saffron in the water until deep gold. Beat together the sugar and egg yolks until thick and creamy. Sieve the cheese into the mixture, and beat with a fork until smooth. Melt the butter and beat it lightly into the cheese mixture, followed by the lemon juice, cream, a pinch of salt, and the saffron liquid. Separately, beat the egg whites to the same consistency as the cheese mixture. Stir 1 tablespoon into the cheese mixture, then fold in the rest. Turn the mixture into the baked flan shell. Bake at 170°C, 325°F, Gas 3, for 1 hour. Cool, Remove the flan ring and serve cold.

Candlelight Cheesecake
Serves 8

Base
60 g (2 oz) butter
175 g (6 oz) plain biscuit or wheat
  crispbread crumbs
30 g (1 oz) castor sugar

Filling and Topping
200 g (7 oz) dried apricots
300 ml ($\frac{1}{2}$ pint) water
60 g (2 oz) walnut pieces
600 g ($1\frac{1}{4}$ lb) full-fat soft cheese
200 g (7 oz) castor sugar
grated rind and juice 1 lemon
2 large eggs
4 tablespoons soured cream
$1\frac{1}{2}$ tablespoons flour
30 g (1 oz) sugar

Soak the apricots for the filling in the water overnight.

Line the base and grease the inside of a 20 cm (8 inch) loose-based cake tin. Melt the butter for the base without letting it get hot. Work in the crumbs and sugar. Press evenly all over the base of the tin. Chill while making the filling.

Drain the apricots and reserve any remaining soaking water. Put aside 90 g (3 oz) of the soaked apricots and chop the rest finely. Grind the walnut pieces coarsely. Mash the cheese until soft and then beat with the castor sugar, lemon rind and juice, eggs and cream until very smooth and creamy. Stir in the flour, chopped apricots and nuts, mixing them in evenly throughout the mixture. Turn the mixture on to the chilled base. Bake at 220°C, 425°F, Gas 7, for 15 minutes. Lower the heat to 180°C, 350°F, Gas 4, and bake for another 45 minutes or until lightly set and slightly browned. Cool in the turned-off oven with the door ajar for 30 minutes. Then remove from the oven and finish cooling in the tin.

While cooling put the reserved 90 g (3 oz) of apricots in a small saucepan with the 30 g (1 oz) of sugar. Measure the soaking liquid and make up to 80 ml (3 fl oz) with water if necessary. Add to the pan and poach the apricots for 10 minutes, or until very soft and syrupy. Cool. Just before serving, pour the apricots and syrup over the centre top of the cheesecake.

Almond Sponge Cheesecake
Serves 8–10

Base
1 tablespoon toasted flaked almonds
  (see page 94)
60 g (2 oz) butter or margarine
100 g ($3\frac{1}{2}$ oz) Marie biscuit crumbs

Filling
3×227 g (8 oz) packets Philadelphia
  soft cheese
4 egg whites
175 g (6 oz) castor sugar
$\frac{1}{2}$ teaspoon vanilla essence
almond essence

Topping
250 ml (8 fl oz) soured cream
1 tablespoon castor sugar
$\frac{1}{2}$ teaspoon vanilla essence
2 tablespoons toasted flaked almonds
  (see page 94)

Line and grease the base of a 20 cm (8 inch) loose-based or springform cake tin about 7.5 cm (3 inches) deep. Crush the nuts and melt the fat gently. Put 2 tablespoons of the biscuit crumbs aside, and mix the rest of the crumbs and the nuts with the melted fat until well blended. Press the mixture evenly all over the base of the cake tin. Dust the sides of the tin with the reserved crumbs. Chill while making the filling.

Bring the cheese up to room temperature and soften thoroughly by mashing it with a fork. Whisk the egg whites until stiff and glossy, gradually adding the sugar, vanilla essence and a few drops of almond essence. Combine with the cheese lightly, and turn on to the chilled base. Bake at 180°C, 350°F, Gas 4, for 25 minutes. While baking, mix together the cream, sugar and vanilla essence for the topping. Spread the sour cream mixture over the hot, baked cheesecake. Raise the oven heat to 240°C, 475°F, Gas 9, return the cheesecake to the oven and bake for 5 minutes only.

Cool the cheesecake in the tin. Sprinkle with the nuts and chill for 2 hours. Run a sharp knife round the edge of the cheesecake to loosen it. Remove from the tin and serve with Melba sauce (see page 92) if desired.

Almond and Cinnamon Cheesecake
Serves 6–8

Base
90 g (3 oz) margarine
150 g (5 oz) fine dry wholemeal breadcrumbs
30 g (1 oz) ground almonds
60 g (2 oz) light soft brown sugar
1½ teaspoons ground cinnamon

Filling
3 eggs, separated
125 g (4 oz) castor sugar
250 g (8 oz) full-fat soft cheese
125 g (4 oz) low-fat soft cheese
grated rind and juice 1 large lemon
80 ml (3 fl oz) double cream
4 tablespoons natural yogurt

Topping
1 teaspoon castor sugar
½ teaspoon ground cinnamon
30 g (1 oz) margarine
2 tablespoons chopped almonds

Melt the margarine in a large frying pan, add the breadcrumbs and stir over gentle heat until they are slightly crisp. Stir in the almonds, sugar and cinnamon. Take off the heat and leave to cool while you line and grease the base of a 20 cm (8 inch) loose-based cake tin. Press the crumb mixture evenly all over the base of the tin.

To make the filling, beat the egg yolks and sugar until thick and pale. Sieve and beat in both cheeses, with the lemon rind and juice. Fold in the cream and yogurt. Whisk the egg whites until they hold soft peaks. Stir 2 tablespoons into the cheese mixture, then fold in the rest. Turn the mixture gently on to the crumb base. Bake at 180°C, 350°F, Gas 4, for 45–50 minutes, or until the cheesecake is just firm in the centre. Cover it loosely with greaseproof paper if it begins to over-brown during cooking.

While baking, make the topping. Mix the sugar and cinnamon, and flake the margarine. When the cheesecake is ready, sprinkle it with the nuts, sugar mixture and flaked margarine. Raise the oven heat to 220°C, 425°F, Gas 7, and return the cheesecake to the oven for a few moments to colour the nuts lightly. Cool in the turned-off oven with the door ajar. Remove from the tin. Leave to firm up for 2–4 hours or longer before serving.

Baked Almond Cheesecake
Serves 6–8

Base
30 g (1 oz) white fat (Trex or Spry)
90 g (3 oz) butter
175 g (6 oz) flour
40 g (1½ oz) ground almonds
40 g (1½ oz) castor sugar
1 egg yolk
1–2 tablespoons cold water

Filling
60 g (2 oz) butter
90 g (3 oz) castor sugar
3 eggs, separated
60 g (2 oz) ground almonds
30 g (1 oz) semolina
250 g (8 oz) full-fat soft cheese
grated rind and juice 1 lemon
90 g (3 oz) seedless raisins

Line the base and grease the inside of a 20 cm (8 inch) loose-based sandwich cake tin or flan ring 4.5 cm (1¾ inches) deep. Make a pastry case as follows: rub the fats into the flour. Add the almonds and sugar and mix. Separately, mix the egg yolk with 1 tablespoon water, add to the dry ingredients, and work lightly into a firm dough, adding the second tablespoon water if needed. Chill for 10 minutes. Roll out on a lightly floured board and use to line the tin. Bake blind (see page 14) at 190°C, 375°F, Gas 5, for 7–8 minutes.

Cream together the butter and sugar for the filling until thick and pale. Beat in the egg yolks one at a time, then beat in the almonds, semolina, cheese, lemon rind and juice. When thoroughly mixed, stir in the raisins. Whisk the egg whites until they hold soft peaks. Stir 2 tablespoons into the cheese mixture, then fold in the rest. Turn the mixture into the partly baked case. Bake at 180°C, 350°F, Gas 4, for 50 minutes, or until the cheesecake is just firm. Cool in the turned-off oven with the door ajar. Either serve while still just warm, or cool completely, and leave for 8–12 hours to firm up before serving. Remove from the tin to serve.

One-Stage Lemon Cottage Cheesecake

Serves 6–8

Base
90 g (3 oz) margarine
175 g (6 oz) digestive biscuit crumbs
40 g (1½ oz) light soft brown sugar
½ teaspoon grated lemon rind

Filling
4 eggs
175 g (6 oz) castor sugar
30 g (1 oz) flour
¼ teaspoon salt
2 tablespoons lemon juice
¼ teaspoon grated lemon rind
100 ml (4 fl oz) double cream
3×226 g (8 oz) cartons cottage cheese

Line the base and grease the inside of a 20 cm (8 inch) loose-based or springform cake tin. Melt the margarine and work it into the crumbs and sugar with the lemon rind. Press the mixture evenly over the base and 2.5 cm (1 inch) of the sides of the tin with the back of a spoon. Chill while making the filling.

Using an electric mixer if possible, beat the eggs until thick, gradually adding the sugar. Beat in the flour and salt. Strain the lemon juice and beat into the mixture with the lemon rind and cream. Sieve the cheese, then beat it in, and continue beating until the mixture is fully blended and smooth. Turn into the chilled tin. Bake at 170°C, 325°F, Gas 3, for 1 hour. Cool in the turned-off oven for another hour then remove and allow to finish cooling in the tin. Run a sharp knife round the inside of the tin to loosen the cheesecake, then remove the tin. Refrigerate for at least 4 hours. Serve with fresh raspberries or strawberries in summer, or with well-drained, canned yellow peaches.

Crumb-Nut Cheesecake

Serves 6–8

Base
90 g (3 oz) butter
175 g (6 oz) dry white breadcrumbs
60 g (2 oz) castor sugar
1½ teaspoons ground cinnamon

Filling
3 eggs, separated
125 g (4 oz) castor sugar
500 g (1 lb) full-fat soft cheese
grated rind and juice 1 lemon
150 ml (¼ pint) soured cream

Topping
1 teaspoon castor sugar
½ teaspoon ground cinnamon
30 g (1 oz) butter
30 g (1 oz) chopped mixed nuts

Melt the butter for the base in a large frying pan, add the breadcrumbs, and stir over gentle heat until golden. Remove from the heat, stir in the sugar and cinnamon, and cool. Meanwhile, line the base and grease the inside of a 20 cm (8 inch) loose-based cake tin. Press about two-thirds of the crumbs evenly all over the base of the tin. Put the remaining crumbs aside.

To make the filling, beat the egg yolks until liquid, add the sugar little by little, beating until creamy. Sieve the cheese and work it in lightly. Mix in the lemon rind and juice, and the cream. Whisk the egg whites until they just hold soft peaks. Stir 2 tablespoons into the cheese mixture, then fold in the rest. Turn the mixture gently on to the crumb base. Bake at 180°C, 350°F, Gas 4, for 45 minutes.

While baking, mix the sugar and cinnamon for the topping, and stir in the reserved crumbs. When the cheesecake is ready, melt the butter for the topping. Sprinkle the crumb mixture, nuts and melted butter over the top of the cheesecake. Return to the oven and bake for another 15 minutes. Cool completely in the turned-off oven with the door ajar, then refrigerate for at least 12 hours. Remove the tin before serving.

Warsaw Sultana Cheesecake

Serves 6–8

Base

    1×23 cm (9 inch) puff pastry flan case,
       baked blind, (see page 14)

Filling

    3 eggs, separated
    60 g (2 oz) castor sugar
    2×226 g (8 oz) cartons cottage cheese
    1 tablespoon cornflour
    $\frac{1}{2}$ teaspoon vanilla essence
    150 ml ($\frac{1}{4}$ pint) soured cream
    60 g (2 oz) sultanas

Topping

    castor or icing sugar

Cool the pastry case if newly baked. Beat the egg yolks and sugar together until thick and pale. Sieve the cheese into a bowl, add the egg-sugar mixture and stir lightly. Separately, blend the cornflour with the vanilla essence and a little of the cream to make a smooth paste. Blend into the cheese mixture, then mix in the remaining cream and the sultanas. Whisk the egg whites until fairly stiff, stir 2 tablespoons into the cheese mixture, then fold in the rest. Pile the filling gently into the pastry case. Bake at 180°C, 350°F, Gas 4, for 55 minutes–1 hour, or until firm in the centre. Cool completely in the turned-off oven. Sprinkle sugar over the top and serve.

Rich Belgian Cheese Flan

Serves 4–6

Base

    1×20 cm (8 inch) puff pastry flan case,
       baked blind, (see page 14)

Filling

    250 g (8 oz) full-fat soft cheese
    2 eggs
    grated rind and juice $\frac{1}{2}$ lemon
    150 ml ($\frac{1}{4}$ pint) double cream
    40 g ($1\frac{1}{2}$ oz) castor sugar

Soften the cheese by working with the back of a spoon. Beat in the eggs, one at a time, until smoothly blended in. Strain the lemon juice and stir it in with the lemon rind, cream and sugar; do not beat in. Turn the mixture into the pastry case, and bake at 180°C, 350°F, Gas 4, for 25 minutes or until the filling is set. Leave to cool completely before serving.

Lattice Peel Cheesecake

Serves 4–6

Base

    125 g (4 oz) flour
    grated rind $\frac{1}{2}$ lemon
    2 teaspoons icing sugar
    salt
    90 g (3 oz) margarine
    1 egg, separated
    1 teaspoon lemon juice

Filling

    30 g (1 oz) chopped mixed peel
    375 g (13 oz) low-fat soft cheese
    grated rind and juice $\frac{1}{2}$ lemon
    60 g (2 oz) castor sugar
    4 tablespoons soured cream
    2 eggs

Grease an 18 cm (7 inch) sandwich layer tin or pie plate. Make a rich pastry with the base ingredients as follows: mix the flour, lemon rind, icing sugar and a small pinch of salt in a bowl. Rub in the margarine as finely as possible. Mix together the egg yolk and lemon juice, and add to the dry ingredients. Work into a firm dough. Chill for at least 15 minutes. Roll out on a lightly floured board and use about two-thirds of the pastry to line the tin or plate. Put the rest aside.

To make the filling, chop the peel if in large pieces. Beat it into the cheese. Add the lemon rind and juice, and the sugar and mix in lightly. Beat the cream into the eggs and blend the liquid with the cheese mixture. Turn the mixture into the pastry case. Make long strips with the reserved pastry, and use them to make a criss-cross lattice pattern on the cheesecake. Seal the edges to the pastry rim with a little of the unused egg white. Brush some of the remaining egg white over the pastry strips. Bake at 200°C, 400°F, Gas 6, for 10 minutes, then reduce the heat to 180°C, 350°F, Gas 4, and bake for a further 30–35 minutes, or until the filling is just firm in the centre. Cool in the tin, and serve cold.

Upside-Down Cheesecake

Serves 6–8

Base

3 tablespoons packeted golden breadcrumbs

Filling

5 eggs, separated
150 g (5 oz) castor sugar
2 tablespoons flour
1 tablespoon semolina
2×226 g (8 oz) cartons cottage cheese
100 ml (4 fl oz) soured cream
grated rind 1 lemon
1 teaspoon vanilla essence

Line the base of a 22 cm (8½ inch) cake tin. Generously grease the inside with butter and sprinkle with the crumbs.

Beat the egg yolks and sugar together in a large bowl until very pale and thick. Sprinkle with the flour and semolina. Sieve the cheese and beat it in, followed by the cream, lemon rind and vanilla essence. Whisk the egg whites until they hold soft peaks and fold them in. Turn the mixture gently into the prepared tin. Bake at 180°C, 350°F, Gas 4, for 1–1¼ hours, until well risen and just firm in the centre. Cool in the turned-off oven for 30 minutes. Take out and run a sharp knife round the edge of the cheesecake, then leave to cool completely. Invert the cooled cake on to a serving plate. Lift off the tin, and peel off the lining paper carefully. The cake will have brownish sides and a peach-coloured top.

Fridge-Fresh Cheesecake

Serves 8

Base

15 g (½ oz) crushed cornflake crumbs

Filling

4×227 g (8 oz) packets Philadelphia soft cheese
grated rind and juice ½ lemon
150 g (5 oz) castor sugar
3 eggs
1 teaspoon vanilla essence

Using butter, generously grease the inside of a 20 cm (8 inch) loose-based cake tin, and coat with the crumbs. Bring the cheese up to room temperature and strain the lemon juice. Put all the filling ingredients in a large bowl and beat briskly until smooth. Turn the mixture gently into the cake tin and stand it in a baking tin containing about 1 cm (½ inch) of water. Bake for 1½ hours at 170°C, 325°F, Gas 3. Cool in the turned-off oven for 30 minutes. Finish cooling in the tin, then chill until needed. The cheesecake will keep for at least 2 weeks, refrigerated. Remove from the tin and decorate as desired before serving.

Hereford Curd Cake

Serves 2–3

Base

90 g (3 oz) shortcrust pastry

Filling

60 g (2 oz) butter
200 g (7 oz) slightly salted home-made milk curd cheese (see page 11), or cottage cheese
1 large egg
2 teaspoons light rum
30 g (1 oz) castor sugar
grated rind 1 small lemon
salt
1 tablespoon currants

Topping

1 teaspoon butter
grated nutmeg

Grease a deep 15 cm (6 inch) patty tin or pie plate. Roll out the pastry on a lightly floured board and use to line tin.

Soften the butter and place in a large bowl. Sieve the cheese into the bowl and beat in the egg, followed by the rum, sugar, lemon rind, a pinch of salt and the currants. Turn the mixture into the pastry case. For the topping, soften the butter. Sprinkle the top of the filling with the nutmeg and dot with the butter. Bake at 190°C, 375°F, Gas 5, for 35 minutes or until the filling is just firm in the centre, and the surface is lightly browned. Cool in the tin. Serve just warm or cold, as a dessert, with apple jelly or stewed apples.

NOTE: this cheesecake stays moist. Do not freeze.

Two-Way Cheesecake (baked)

Two-Way Cheesecake

(rich or light, baked or unbaked)
Serves 6–8

Base

60 g (2 oz) butter
250 g (8 oz) digestive biscuit crumbs
30 g (1 oz) castor sugar
1½ teaspoons ground cinnamon

Filling

2 tablespoons cold water · for an unbaked cheesecake
1 packet (15 g/½ oz) gelatine · for an unbaked cheesecake
3 eggs, separated
125 g (4 oz) castor sugar
350 g (12 oz) full-fat soft cheese
   (for a rich cake), or cottage cheese
   (for a light cake)
grated rind and juice 1 lemon
150 ml (¼ pint) double cream (for a rich
   cake), or single cream (for a light cake)
30 g (1 oz) chopped mixed nuts (for a
   baked cheesecake)
walnut halves, glacé cherries, angelica
   leaves and whipped cream for
   decorating an unbaked cheesecake (optional)

Line the base and generously grease the inside of an 18 cm (7 inch) loose-based cake tin. Melt the butter and work in 175 g (6 oz) of the crumbs, with the sugar and cinnamon. Press evenly all over the base of the tin. Coat the sides of the tin with the remaining, dry crumbs. Chill while making the filling.

For an unbaked cheesecake, put the water in a small heatproof bowl, sprinkle on the gelatine and allow to soften. Stand the bowl in a pan of very hot water, and stir until the gelatine dissolves. Leave to cool to tepid. Meanwhile beat the egg yolks and sugar together in a second heatproof bowl until well blended. Place the bowl over a pan of simmering water, and whisk until the mixture is light and creamy. Remove from the heat and continue whisking until the mixture has cooled to tepid. Sieve the cheese and stir it in with the lemon rind and juice. Whip the cream until it just holds soft peaks, and stir it lightly into the cheese mixture. Whisk the egg whites to a soft foam. Stir the cooled gelatine into the cheese mixture slowly, taking care that no lumps form, then fold in the egg whites. Turn the mixture gently on to the crumb base, and chill until set. Remove from the tin, and decorate as you wish just before serving.

For a baked cheesecake, beat the egg yolks and sugar together until thick and creamy. Sieve the cheese and beat it in with the lemon rind and juice, and the cream. Whisk the egg whites to a soft foam. Fold them into the mixture. Bake at 170°C, 325°F, Gas 3, for 45 minutes. Sprinkle the nuts on top, and bake for another 15–20 minutes. Cool in the turned-off oven with the door ajar. When cold, remove from the tin and leave in a cool place for 2 hours to firm up before serving.

Alpine Cheesecake
Serves 6–8

Base

1×20 cm (8 inch) pastry flan case,
  baked blind, (see page 14)

Filling

175 g (6 oz) Gruyère cheese
30 g (1 oz) self-raising flour
90 g (3 oz) castor sugar
grated rind and juice 1 lemon
1 egg yolk
5 tablespoons natural yogurt
2 egg whites

Any type of pastry is suitable for this cheesecake. Grate the cheese into a large bowl, add the flour, sugar and lemon rind, and mix thoroughly. Separately, beat the egg yolk lightly, then stir it gently into the yogurt. Strain the lemon juice and stir into the egg-yogurt mixture. Mix gently but thoroughly with the dry ingredients. Whisk the egg whites until stiff but not dry. Stir 1 tablespoon into the cheese mixture, then fold in the rest. Turn the mixture gently into the pastry case set on a heavy baking sheet. Bake at 170°C, 325°F, Gas 3, for 35–45 minutes, or until firm in the centre. Cool in the turned-off oven with the door ajar for 10–15 minutes, then finish cooling on a wire rack. Serve cold.

Alpine Cheesecake

Italian Cheesecake or Flan
Serves 6

Base
40 g (1½ oz) butter
40 g (1½ oz) margarine
30 g (1 oz) icing sugar
1 egg yolk
ground cinnamon
150 g (5 oz) flour

Filling
15 g (½ oz) Parmesan cheese
350 g (12 oz) cottage cheese
1 egg
15 g (½ oz) flour
30 g (1 oz) castor sugar
2 tablespoons natural yogurt
grated rind and juice ½ lemon
salt, ground cinnamon

Topping
icing sugar
ground cinnamon

Grease the inside of an 18 cm (7 inch) flan ring set on a lined baking sheet. Make the pastry the day before it is wanted as follows: soften the fats. Cream together the softened fats and icing sugar, then mix in thoroughly the egg yolk, a pinch of cinnamon and the flour. Gather into a ball, and chill for 30 minutes. Then press the mixture, which will still be quite soft, evenly all over the inside of the flan ring to make a case. Trim the top, and brush off any loose fragments. Chill overnight.

To make the filling, first grate the Parmesan cheese, then sieve together, or process in an electric blender, both cheeses, the egg, flour, sugar, yogurt, lemon rind and juice, and a pinch each of salt and cinnamon. Turn the mixture into the chilled case. Bake at 150°C, 300°F, Gas 2, for about 45 minutes or until just firm in the centre. Cool in the turned-off oven with the door ajar. Sprinkle with icing sugar and a pinch of cinnamon just before serving.

Luxemburg Kaes Kuch (Cheesecake)
Serves 6

Base
250 g (8 oz) flour
2 teaspoons baking powder
¼ teaspoon salt
1 tablespoon castor sugar
125 g (4 oz) butter
175–200 ml (5–6 fl oz) milk

Filling
500 g (1 lb) unsalted home-made
    milk curd cheese (see page 11 and note below)
3 eggs, separated
100 ml (4 fl oz) double cream
grated rind and juice ½ lemon
125 g (4 oz) castor sugar
¼ teaspoon salt

Grease the inside of an 18 cm (7 inch) loose-based sandwich cake tin. Sift the flour, baking powder and salt for the base into a bowl. Mix in the sugar. Rub in the butter lightly. Mix to a springy dough with the milk. Roll out or pat the dough into the right shape to line the tin.

To make the filling, beat the cheese until smooth. Beat in the egg yolks, one at a time. Then stir in the cream, lemon rind and juice. Lastly, mix in 90 g (3 oz) of the sugar, putting the rest aside. Mix well. Turn into the pastry case and bake at 190°C, 375°F, Gas 5, for 35 minutes or until the cheesecake is just firm.

Shortly before the end of the cooking time whisk the egg whites and salt together until stiff, adding half of the remaining sugar. Continue whisking until the meringue is stiff and glossy. Fold in the last of the sugar. Reduce the oven heat to 150°C, 300°F, Gas 2. Remove the cheesecake and pile the meringue on top, taking care to cover the filling mixture completely. Return to the oven and bake until the meringue is set and lightly browned. Remove from the tin and serve warm or cool.

NOTE: unsalted soft curd cheese is available from health food stores if you do not make your own.

Meringue-Topped Cheesecake

Serves 6–8

Base
1 egg
30 g (1 oz) castor sugar
30 g (1 oz) flour

Filling
250 g (8 oz) full-fat soft cheese
75 g (2½ oz) castor sugar
salt
1 tablespoon flour
½ teaspoon vanilla essence
grated rind ½ lemon
2 egg yolks
5 tablespoons double cream
1 teaspoon milk

Topping
2 egg whites
¼ teaspoon cream of tartar
60 g (2 oz) castor sugar

Thoroughly grease the base of a 23 cm (9 inch) flan case or ring on a baking sheet. Beat together the egg and sugar until thick and pale. Fold in the flour and spread the mixture evenly over the base. Bake at 200°C, 400°F, Gas 6, for 10–12 minutes, until cooked through and slightly shrunk from the sides of the case or ring. Cool.

For the filling, mash the cheese with a fork until soft. Beat in the sugar, a pinch of salt, the flour, vanilla essence and lemon rind. Separately, beat together the egg yolks, cream and milk until the egg yolks are liquid and blended in. Then stir into the cheese mixture and beat until smooth. Turn the mixture on to the cooled sponge base in the case or ring.

For the topping, beat the egg whites and cream of tartar until stiff, adding the sugar gradually while beating. Pile the meringue all over the cheese mixture. Bake at 180°C, 350°F, Gas 4, for 25–30 minutes or until the meringue is lightly browned. Cool completely in the turned-off oven. Serve with whipped, sweetened double cream.

Milk Curd Cheesecake

Serves 4–6

Base
60 g (2 oz) digestive biscuit crumbs
2 teaspoons castor sugar
30 g (1 oz) butter

Filling
125 g (4 oz) home-made milk curd cheese
   (see page 11)
60 g (2 oz) butter
grated rind and juice ½ lemon
1 teaspoon orange juice
2 eggs, separated
60 g (2 oz) ground almonds
60 g (2 oz) castor sugar
2 tablespoons self-raising flour

This cheesecake is prepared and baked upside down, and inverted just before serving.

Line the base and grease with butter the inside of an 18 cm (7 inch) sandwich cake tin. Put the cheese in a bowl and break it up with a fork. Melt the butter without letting it get hot. Strain the lemon and orange juice together. Stir the butter, lemon rind, fruit juices and egg yolks into the cheese, followed by the almonds and sugar. Beat the mixture until well blended. Sift the flour and fold into the mixture. Whisk the egg whites until stiff but not dry, and fold in lightly. Turn the mixture into the prepared tin.

Mix the crumbs with the sugar. Melt the butter and combine with the dry ingredients to make a crumbly mixture. Scatter it lightly and evenly over the filling. Bake at 220°C, 425°F, Gas 7, for 10 minutes, then reduce the heat to 180°C, 350°F, Gas 4, and bake for another 20 minutes, or until the cheesecake is firm and dry in the centre when pierced with a thin skewer. Cover loosely with greaseproof paper if the crumbs begin to over-brown while baking.

Loosen the cheesecake from the sides of the tin with a flexible spatula or palette knife, then leave to cool in the tin. Invert gently on to a serving plate so that the crumbs form the base. Peel off the lining paper. Serve cut in wedges.

Sweet Brie Cheesecake

Serves 8–10

Base

    125 g (4 oz) butter
    125 g (4 oz) flour
    60 g (2 oz) castor sugar

Filling

    2×227 g (8 oz) packets Philadelphia soft cheese
    200 g (7 oz) soft Brie cheese
    1 tablespoon flour
    90 g (3 oz) castor sugar
    4 eggs, separated
    100 ml (4 fl oz) double cream
    1 teaspoon vanilla essence
    ¼ teaspoon salt

To make the case, separately grease the base and sides of a 23 cm (9 inch) loose-based cake tin about 7.5 cm (3 inches) deep. Soften the butter. Mix together the flour and sugar, and work in the butter to make a soft dough. Spread half the dough evenly over the base of the tin. Bake at 200°C, 400°F, Gas 6, for 8 minutes, until lightly browned. Cool. Fit the base and sides of the tin together. Spread the remaining dough over 5 cm (2 inches) of the sides of the tin, to form a shell. Chill while making the filling.

Bring the cheeses up to room temperature and remove the rind from the Brie. Beat together until very smooth and creamy. Beat in the flour and sugar. Beat in the egg yolks, one at a time, followed by the cream and vanilla essence. Separately, beat the egg whites and salt until fairly stiff. Fold into the creamy cheese mixture. Pour into the chilled case and bake at 180°C, 350°F, Gas 4, for 45 minutes. Turn off the oven and leave the cheesecake for 45 minutes longer. Then remove from the oven and cool in the tin. Remove the tin, and chill for at least 2 hours before serving.

Sweet Brie Cheesecake

Maryland Party Cheesecake (with Blackcurrant Purée)

Maryland Party Cheesecake
Serves 10–12

Base
100 g (3½ oz) butter
60 g (2 oz) light soft brown sugar
250 g (8 oz) Rich Tea biscuit
   crumbs
¼ teaspoon ground cinnamon
¼ teaspoon grated nutmeg

Filling
4 eggs, separated
250 ml (8 fl oz) soured cream
1 teaspoon vanilla essence
250 g (8 oz) castor sugar
60 g (2 oz) flour
¼ teaspoon salt
500 g (1 lb) full-fat soft cheese

Line the base and grease the inside of a 23 cm (9 inch) loose-based cake tin. Melt the butter without letting it get hot. Sieve the sugar into a bowl, add the crumbs, cinnamon and nutmeg, mix, and then work into the butter. Press the crumb mixture evenly all over the base and 2.5 cm (1 inch) of the sides of the cake tin. Chill while making the filling.

Beat the egg yolks until thick, and beat in the cream and vanilla essence. Mix 175 g (6 oz) of the sugar with the flour and salt, and beat into the egg-cream mixture little by little. Beat in the cheese a little at a time. Whisk the egg whites until fairly stiff, adding the remaining sugar while doing so. Fold into the cheese mixture. Turn gently into the chilled case and bake at 170°C, 325°F, Gas 3, for 1 hour. Cool in the turned-off oven with the door ajar. Remove from the tin, and chill for at least 1 hour before serving. Serve with a sweet fruit sauce (see pages 92–94).

Creamy Crowd Cheesecake
Serves 12

Base and Topping
175 g (6 oz) crushed cornflake crumbs
40 g (1½ oz) castor sugar
90 g (3 oz) soft tub margarine
Filling
3×227 g (8 oz) packets Philadelphia soft cheese
1×200 g (7 oz) can sweetened condensed milk
4 eggs, separated
300 ml (½ pint) soured cream
1 tablespoon castor sugar
1 teaspoon vanilla essence
1 teaspoon grated orange rind
½ teaspoon salt

Line the base and grease the inside of a 25 cm (10 inch) springform cake tin. Mix the crumbs and sugar with the margarine to make a mixture like bread-crumbs. Put half aside. Press the rest evenly over the base of the tin.

To make the filling, first bring the cheese up to room temperature. Then, using an electric mixer if possible, beat the cheese and condensed milk together until smooth. Add the yolks one at a time, blending each in thoroughly. When completely blended, beat in the cream, sugar, vanilla essence and orange rind. Separately beat the egg whites with the salt until they hold soft peaks. Fold them into the cheese mixture. Turn gently into the cake tin and sprinkle the top with the reserved crumb mixture. Bake at 150°C, 300°F, Gas 2, for 1¼–2 hours, or until a skewer run into the centre of the cake comes out clean. Cool in the turned-off oven with the door ajar. Leave in the tin until quite cold.

Serve this golden-topped cheesecake with double the recipe quantity of apricot sauce (see page 93) in a separate jug.

Creamy Walnut Cheesecake
Serves 10

Base and Topping
30 g (1 oz) walnut pieces
200 g (7 oz) digestive biscuit crumbs
½ teaspoon ground cinnamon
100 g (3½ oz) butter or margarine
Filling
2×227 g (8 oz) packets Philadelphia soft cheese
2 large eggs
175 g (6 oz) castor sugar
¼ teaspoon salt
2 teaspoons vanilla essence
¼ teaspoon almond essence
400 ml (¾ pint) soured cream

Line the base and grease the inside of a shallow 20 cm (8 inch) loose-based sandwich cake tin. Finely chop the nuts. Mix together the crumbs, nuts and cinnamon. Melt the fat and work the dry ingredients into it. Put 3 tablespoons of the crumb-nut mixture aside for the topping, and press the rest evenly all over the base of the tin. Chill while making the filling.

First bring the cheese up to room temperature. Beat the eggs until liquid. Gradually, beat them into the cheese. Add the sugar, salt and both essences. Beat until smooth. Stir in the cream, and pour the mixture on to the chilled base. Bake at 190°C, 375°F, Gas 5, for 25–30 minutes or until just set in the centre. Cool in the turned-off oven with the door ajar for 30 minutes. Remove from the oven and finish cooling completely in the tin, then chill for 12–18 hours before use. To serve, remove from the tin and sprinkle with the reserved crumbs and nuts. This cheesecake remains soft and creamy inside.

Light Cream Cheesecake
Serves 8–10

Base and Topping
175 g (6 oz) water biscuit crumbs
30 g 1 (oz) castor sugar
¼ teaspoon ground cinnamon
1 tablespoon butter or margarine

Filling
500 g (1 lb) full-fat soft cheese
2 tablespoons flour
90 g (3 oz) castor sugar
salt
¼ teaspoon vanilla essence
4 eggs, separated
250 ml (8 fl oz) single cream
grated rind 1 lemon

Line the base and grease the inside of a 23 cm (9 inch) loose-based cake tin. Make sure the crumbs are crushed finely and evenly, and mix them with the sugar and cinnamon. Soften the fat and gradually work it into the dry ingredients. Put aside a quarter of the crumb mixture and press the rest, in a thin even layer, over the base of the tin. Chill while making the filling.

Using an electric mixer if possible, blend the cheese, flour, sugar, a pinch of salt and the vanilla essence. Add the egg yolks one at a time, blending well each time. Then beat in the cream and lemon rind. Separately, whisk the egg whites until stiff, then fold them into the cheese mixture. Turn the mixture into the cake tin, and sprinkle with the reserved crumb mixture. Bake at 170°C, 325°F, Gas 3, for 1 hour, or until a skewer run into the centre of the cake comes out clean. Cool in the tin. Run a sharp knife round the inside of the tin to loosen the cheesecake, then remove the sides of the tin. Since this cheesecake is fragile serve it from the base of the cake tin.

Cinnamon Cheesecake with Sour Cream Topping
Serves 4–6

Base
8 slices bought honey cake
Filling
60 g (2 oz) butter
1 tablespoon cornflour
2 tablespoons milk
500 g (1 lb) low-fat soft cheese
½ teaspoon vanilla essence
2 eggs, separated
1 tablespoon castor sugar

Topping
1 teaspoon castor sugar
150 ml (¼ pint) soured cream
ground cinnamon

Line the base and grease the inside of an 18 cm (7 inch) loose-based square cake tin. Cover the base with the cake slices in one even layer.

Heat the oven to 230°C, 450°F, Gas 8. For the filling, melt the butter without letting it get hot. Blend the cornflour into the milk smoothly. When blended beat into the cheese with the butter and vanilla essence. Then beat in the egg yolks, and continue beating until the cheese mixture is light and fluffy. Whisk the egg whites until fairly stiff and glossy, gradually adding the sugar, and then fold into the cheesecake mixture. Turn the mixture gently on to the cake base, and level the top with a palette knife. Put into the oven and immediately reduce the heat to 180°C, 350°F, Gas 4, and bake for 25 minutes. While baking, mix the sugar for the topping into the cream.

Remove the cheesecake from the oven and turn up the heat to 220°C, 425°F, Gas 7. Spread the soured cream mixture very gently over the filling, sprinkle on a little cinnamon and return to the oven. Bake for 10 minutes. Remove, and cool in the tin. Cover with foil and refrigerate for at least 12 hours before serving. The cake will keep for up to 48 hours.

Chiffon Cheesecake (with Plum Topping)

Chiffon Cheesecake

Serves 8–10

Base
 125 g (4 oz) butter
 250 g (8 oz) Marie biscuit crumbs
Filling
 3×226 g (8 oz) cartons cottage cheese
 2 tablespoons lemon juice
 175 g (6 oz) castor sugar
 40 g ($\frac{1}{2}$ oz) flour
 $\frac{1}{4}$ teaspoon salt
 1 teaspoon vanilla essence
 3 eggs, separated
 225 ml (7 fl oz) whipping cream

Line the base and grease the inside of a 23 cm (9 inch) loose-based cake tin. Melt the butter and work it into the crumbs. Press evenly over the base and 5 cm (2 inches) of the sides of the cake tin to make a shell. Chill while making the filling.

Sieve the cheese and strain the lemon juice. Using an electric mixer if possible, combine the cheese with 125 g (4 oz) of the sugar. Beat in the flour, salt, lemon juice and vanilla essence. Separately, beat the egg yolks until thick, then mix them in. Whip the cream until it holds soft peaks and whisk it into the mixture. Lastly, whisk the egg whites until fairly stiff, adding the remaining sugar while doing so, and fold in. Turn the mixture gently into the chilled case. Bake slowly, at 150°C, 300°F, Gas 2, for 1–1$\frac{1}{4}$ hours. Cool the cheesecake in the turned-off oven for another hour. Then remove from the oven and finish cooling in the tin. Remove from the tin and chill for 8–12 hours before use. Decorate with a fruit topping (see pages 92–94) if desired.

Rich Natural Cheesecake (Picture: Billingtons Natural Brown Sugars)

Rich Natural Cheesecake

Serves 10–12

Base
90 g (3 oz) butter
150 g (5 oz) granary or wholemeal
   breadcrumbs
30 g (1 oz) ground almonds
60 g (2 oz) light muscovado sugar

Filling
100 g (3½ oz) butter
2×226 g (8 oz) cartons cottage cheese
500 g (1 lb) full-fat soft cheese
250 g (8 oz) light muscovado sugar
4 eggs
5 tablespoons wholemeal flour
3 tablespoons arrowroot
¼ teaspoon ground cinnamon
2 tablespoons lemon juice
1½ teaspoons vanilla essence
300 ml (½ pint) soured cream

Topping
40 g (1½ oz) demerara sugar

Line the base and grease the inside of a 23 cm (9 inch) loose-based cake tin about 7.5 cm (3 inches) deep. Melt the butter and mix with the breadcrumbs, almonds and sugar. Press the mixture evenly all over the base of the tin. Chill while making the filling.

Melt the butter and allow to cool. Sieve the cottage cheese into a large bowl. Beat both cheeses together for 2 minutes. Still beating, add the sugar gradually, then the eggs, one at a time, followed by the flour, arrowroot, cinnamon, lemon juice and vanilla essence. Separately, mix together the cooled butter and the cream, and stir them into the cheese mixture. Pour the mixture into the tin, and bake for 1¾ hours at 170°C, 325°F, Gas 3. Cool in the turned-off oven for 2½ hours, then leave the door ajar until the cheesecake is cold. Refrigerate for 12–18 hours before use. Before serving, remove from the tin and sprinkle with the sugar.

This light, rich party cheesecake uses only organic ingredients.

Soured Cream Cheesecake

Serves 10–12

Base

100 g (3½ oz) self-raising flour
125 g (4 oz) butter
125 g (4 oz) castor sugar
2 eggs
1 tablespoon milk
1 teaspoon vanilla essence

Filling

250 g (8 oz) low-fat soft cheese, or use half
 low-fat and half full-fat soft cheese
125 g (4 oz) castor sugar
100 ml (4 fl oz) soured cream
1 teaspoon vanilla essence
2 eggs

Topping

250 ml (8 fl oz) soured cream
30 g (1 oz) castor sugar
1 teaspoon vanilla essence

Make the filling before the base, as follows. Beat the cheese until soft and smooth, adding the sugar. Beat in the cream and vanilla essence, then the eggs, one at a time. Beat until well blended, then put aside and make the base.

Line the base and grease the inside of a 25 cm (10 inch) loose-based sandwich cake tin or flan case at least 5 cm (2 inches) deep. Sprinkle a little of the flour on the bottom. Cream together the butter and sugar until light and fluffy. Beat in the eggs, one at a time, then stir in the milk and vanilla essence. Beat or stir in the remaining flour, and blend thoroughly. Spread the batter over the base and sides of the tin or case, more thickly on the base. Spoon in the filling mixture. Bake at 170°C, 325°F, Gas 3, for 1 hour.

While baking, stir together the ingredients for the topping. When the cheesecake is cooked, spoon the topping over the filling and return to the oven for 5 minutes. Cool in the turned-off oven with the door ajar for 10 minutes only, then finish cooling at room temperature. Refrigerate for at least 4 hours before serving.

Lindy's Original Cheesecake

Serves 12–14

Base

125 g (4 oz) flour
40 g (1½ oz) castor sugar
1 teaspoon grated lemon rind
¼ teaspoon vanilla essence
1 egg yolk
60 g (2 oz) butter

Filling

1 kg (2 lb) low-fat soft cheese
250 g (8 oz) full-fat soft cheese
275 g (9 oz) castor sugar
30 g (1 oz) flour
1½ teaspoons grated orange rind
1½ teaspoons grated lemon rind
¼ teaspoon vanilla essence
5 eggs
2 egg yolks
4 tablespoons double cream

Sift the flour into a bowl, add the sugar and lemon rind and mix. Make a well in the centre and add the vanilla essence, egg yolk and butter. Work together quickly with your hands to make a dough. Wrap in waxed paper and chill for 1 hour. Oil the base (without the sides) of a deep 22 cm (8½ inch) loose-based or springform cake tin. Roll out the dough 3 mm (⅛ inch) thick on a floured board. Lay part of the pastry sheet on the base, and trim off by running the rolling pin over the sharp edges. Bake the pastry circle at 200°C, 400°F, Gas 6, for 8–10 minutes or until firm and lightly coloured. Cool. Grease the sides of the tin and fit them in place over the base. Roll out the unused pastry into a wide strip 3 mm (⅛ inch) thick and use it to line the greased sides of the tin.

To make the filling, beat both cheeses together until soft and well blended. Mix in the sugar, flour, grated orange and lemon rind and vanilla essence. Stir in the eggs and egg yolks, one at a time, stirring lightly after each addition. Stir in the cream. Turn the mixture into the pastry case. Bake in a very hot oven, at 240°C, 475°F, Gas 9, for 10 minutes. Reduce the heat to 110°C, 225°F, Gas ¼, and continue baking for 1 hour. Remove from the oven and cool in the tin, removing it just before serving. Eat the cheesecake within 12 hours of making it.

NOTE: this recipe was given to the author by Lindy's restaurant in New York, U.S.A. in 1962.

Brandied Apricot Cheesecake

Serves 8

Base

90 g (3 oz) flour
90 g (3 oz) self-raising flour
1 teaspoon ground cinnamon
90 g (3 oz) butter
1 tablespoon castor sugar
1 egg yolk
2 tablespoons cold water

Filling

500 g (1 lb) full-fat soft cheese
4 eggs
150 g (5 oz) castor sugar
1 teaspoon vanilla essence
100 ml (4 fl oz) soured cream
2 tablespoons self-raising flour

Topping

60 g (2 oz) dried apricots
1 tablespoon castor sugar
brandy to cover
whipped cream to decorate

Line the base and grease the inside of a 20 cm (8 inch) loose-based sandwich cake tin. Sift both quantities of flour and the cinnamon into a mixing bowl. Rub in the butter until the mixture is like fine breadcrumbs. Stir in the sugar. Separately, beat the egg yolk with the water, and mix into the dry ingredients to make a smooth dough. Add a very little extra water if needed. Roll out on a lightly floured board and use to line the cake tin. Chill while making the filling.

Beat the cheese until very soft and smooth. Separately, beat the eggs until frothy, then beat in the sugar little by litle, blending completely. Beat in the vanilla essence and cream. Gradually beat the cheese into the egg mixture, blending each addition in smoothly without leaving lumps. Sprinkle with the flour and incorporate it with one last quick beating. Turn the mixture into the chilled pastry case. Bake at 180°C, 350°F, Gas 4, for 30 minutes. Lower the heat to 150°C, 300°F, Gas 2, and bake for another 15 minutes or until the filling is lightly set. Cool for 20 minutes in the turned-off oven with the door ajar. Then remove from the oven and finish cooling at room temperature. When cool remove from the tin and then refrigerate for 24 hours before topping and serving.

Make the topping while refrigerating the cheesecake. Put the apricots and sugar in a bowl, mix well and cover with brandy. Leave overnight.

Then sieve all three ingredients, or process briefly in an electric blender, to obtain a smooth purée. Spread lightly on the cheesecake just before serving and top with rosettes of whipped cream.

Cheddar Cheesecake

Serves 6–8

Base

1×20 cm (8 inch) shortcrust pastry
flan case, baked blind, (see page 14)

Filling

175 g (6 oz) mild Cheddar cheese
grated rind and juice 1 lemon
30 g (1 oz) self-raising flour
90 g (3 oz) castor sugar
1 egg, separated
5 tablespoons natural yogurt
1 egg white

Grate the cheese into a large bowl, add the lemon rind, flour and sugar and mix thoroughly. Separately, beat the egg yolk lightly and gently stir in the yogurt. Strain and stir in the lemon juice. Mix the liquid into the dry ingredients little by little, to make a smooth mixture. Whisk both egg whites together until fairly stiff. Stir 1 tablespoon into the cheese mixture, then fold in the rest lightly but thoroughly. Turn gently into the flan case set on a baking sheet. Bake at 170°C, 325°F, Gas 3, for 35–45 minutes or until firm in the centre and lightly browned. Cool on the baking sheet. Serve cold.

Plum Cheesecake

Plum Cheesecake

Serves 6

Base

30 g (1 oz) margarine or butter
140 g (4½ oz) digestive biscuit crumbs
250 g (8 oz) fresh, stewed or canned plums

Filling

1 × 227 g (8 oz) packet Philadelphia soft cheese
60 g (2 oz) margarine
2 tablespoons clear honey
150 ml (¼ pint) soured cream
2 eggs, separated
grated rind and juice 1 lemon

Topping

150 ml (¼ pint) natural yogurt
1 tablespoon clear honey
1 tablespoon lemon juice

Line the base and grease the inside of a 23 cm (9 inch) loose-based cake tin. Melt the fat and work in the crumbs. Press the mixture evenly over the base of the tin. Stone the plums and place on top of the base. Chill while making the filling.

First bring the cheese up to room temperature. Cream the margarine and honey together until light and fluffy. Gradually beat in the cheese, cream, egg yolks, lemon rind and juice. Whisk the egg whites until stiff and fold into the cheese mixture. Pour on to the prepared base and bake for 1 hour at 180°C, 350°F, Gas 4, until set and turning golden-brown. Reduce the oven to 150°C, 300°F, Gas 2.

For the topping beat together the yogurt, honey and lemon juice. Pour over the top of the cheesecake and smooth with a palette knife. Bake for a further 15 minutes until set. Cool in the turned-off oven with the door ajar for 30 minutes. Remove the tin before serving.

Strawberry-Topped Cheesecake (page 38)

Strawberry-Topped Cheesecake

(Picture page 37)
Serves 8–10

Base
125 g (4 oz) butter
125 g (4 oz) flour
40 g (1½ oz) castor sugar
1 teaspoon grated lemon rind
1 egg yolk

Filling
350 g (12 oz) full-fat soft cheese
250 g (8 oz) low-fat soft cheese
125 g (4 oz) castor sugar
1½ tablespoons flour
1 teaspoon grated lemon rind
¼ teaspoon vanilla essence
3 eggs
1 egg yolk
2 tablespoons double cream

Topping
8 fresh strawberries
fresh strawberry topping (see page 94)

Line the base and grease the inside of a 23 cm (9 inch) loose-based cake tin. Soften the butter. Mix together the flour, sugar and lemon rind, and work in the butter and egg yolk to make a smooth, soft, pasty dough. With the back of a spoon, pat or spread the dough over the base and about 5 cm (2 inches) of the sides of the tin. Bake at 200°C, 400°F, Gas 6, for 7–8 minutes. Cool whilst making the filling.

Using an electric mixer if possible, beat both cheeses together until creamy. Beat in the sugar, flour, lemon rind, vanilla essence and eggs. Separately, blend the extra egg yolk into the cream, then beat into the cheese mixture. Pour into the cooled shell. Bake at 140°C, 275°F, Gas 1, for 1½–2 hours or until just set. Cool in the turned-off oven for 1 hour, then remove from oven and allow to cool completely. While cooling make up half the recipe quantity of fresh strawberry topping (see page 94) and allow to cool. When cheesecake is completely cold, halve the strawberries and arrange on top. Spoon the cold topping over the strawberries, covering the cheesecake. Chill for at least 1 hour before serving.

Fruit-Topped Vanilla Cheesecake

Serves 4–6

Base
flour as required
90 g (3 oz) digestive biscuit crumbs

Filling
500 g (1 lb) full-fat or low-fat
    soft cheese
3 eggs, separated
125 g (4 oz) castor sugar
30 g (1 oz) cornflour
½ teaspoon vanilla essence
150 ml (¼ pint) soured cream

Topping
1×219 g (7¾ oz) can fruit salad in syrup
80 ml (3 fl oz) fresh orange juice
1 teaspoon arrowroot

Generously grease the base of an 18 cm (7 inch) loose-based cake tin. Sprinkle with flour. Cover with the crumbs, and press down well to make a firm layer.

To make the filling, sieve the cheese. Beat the egg yolks in a bowl until thick and pale. Stir in the cheese. Mix the sugar and cornflour, then stir them into the mixture. Add the vanilla essence and cream. Beat until smooth. Whisk the egg whites until they hold soft peaks. Stir 2 tablespoons into the cheese mixture, then fold in the rest. Turn gently on to the crumb base, and bake at 180°C, 350°F, Gas 4, for 1 hour. Cool in the turned-off oven for another 15–20 minutes. Remove from the oven and finish cooling in the tin.

Drain the can of fruit over a basin. Strain the orange juice into a measuring jug, and add enough syrup from the can to make 150 ml (¼ pint) of liquid. Mix a little with the arrowroot to make a smooth cream, then mix the arrowroot cream into the liquid. Put the mixture in a small saucepan, bring to the boil, and stir until the liquid thickens. Cool until almost cold. Remove the cheesecake from the tin. Arrange the fruit attractively on top of the cheesecake and spoon the fruit glaze over it. Chill before serving.

Pineapple Cheesecake
Serves 8

Base and Topping
90 g (3 oz) butter
250 g (8 oz) gingernut crumbs
1×376 g (13¼ oz) can crushed pineapple
   in syrup
Filling
250 g (8 oz) full-fat soft cheese
250 g (8 oz) low-fat soft cheese
3 eggs, separated
140 g (4½ oz) castor sugar
30 g (1 oz) flour
½ teaspoon salt
1×170 g (6 oz) can unsweetened
   evaporated milk
½ teaspoon vanilla essence

Line the base and grease the inside of a 23 cm (9 inch) loose-based cake tin. Melt the butter and work in the crumbs. Press the mixture evenly over the base and 2.5 cm (1 inch) of the sides of the tin. Bake at 170°C, 325°F, Gas 3, for 10 minutes. While baking, drain the pineapple thoroughly, reserving the syrup. Cool the baked shell, then spread it evenly with 125 g (4 oz) of the drained, crushed pineapple. Put the rest aside.

Beat the cheeses together until very soft, then beat in the egg yolks, 90 g (3 oz) of the sugar, the flour and the salt. Beat until very smooth, then beat in the evaporated milk, 1 tablespoon reserved pineapple syrup and the vanilla essence. Separately, whisk the egg whites until semi-stiff, gradually whisking in the rest of the sugar. Fold into the cheese mixture. Pour into the chilled case. Bake at 170°C, 325°F, Gas 3, for 1 hour. Cool in the turned-off oven. When cool, remove and chill for at least 2 hours. Before serving, remove from the tin and decorate with pineapple topping (see page 92) made with the remaining crushed pineapple, and substituting 2 tablespoons reserved syrup for the water.

Teatime Fruit Yogurt Cheesecake
Serves 6–8

Base
90 g (3 oz) butter
150 g (5 oz) dry white breadcrumbs
30 g (1 oz) ground almonds
60 g (2 oz) castor sugar
1–2 drops almond essence
Filling
3 eggs, separated
125 g (4 oz) castor sugar
350 g (12 oz) low-fat soft cheese
grated rind and juice 1 small lemon
4 tablespoons double cream
80 ml (3 fl oz) fruit-flavoured
   yogurt, (peach, pineapple or raspberry)
Topping
icing sugar

Melt the butter in a large frying pan and stir in the breadcrumbs. Continue stirring until they are evenly golden-brown and beginning to crisp. Take off the heat, and stir in the almonds, sugar and almond essence. Cool while you line and grease the base and sides of a 20 cm (8 inch) loose-based cake tin. Press the crumbs firmly in an even layer on the base of the tin. Chill.

To make the filling, beat the egg yolks and sugar together until thick and creamy. Sieve in the cheese, then beat it in with the lemon rind and juice. Fold in the cream and yogurt. Separately, whisk the egg whites until they hold soft peaks. Stir 2 tablespoons into the cheese mixture, then fold in the rest. Turn the mixture gently on to the chilled base. Bake at 180°C, 350°F, Gas 4, for 45–50 minutes until the cheesecake is just firm in the centre. Cover loosely with greaseproof paper if it begins to over-brown while baking.

Cool the cheesecake in the tin. When cold, remove the sides of the tin and the lining paper. Loosen the cheesecake from the base of the tin with a sharp knife, and slide it carefully on to a serving plate. Dust with icing sugar and serve.

Greek Honey Cheesecake

Serves 6–8

Base

350 g (12 oz) flour
1½ teaspoons baking powder
salt
150 g (5 oz) butter
2–4 tablespoons cold water

Filling

750 g (1½ lb) myzithra or low-fat
   soft cheese (see note below)
150 g (5 oz) castor sugar
1 teaspoon ground cinnamon
250 g (8 oz) clear honey
5 eggs

Grease a 20 cm (8 inch) pie plate, or flan ring on a baking sheet. Sift the flour, baking powder and a pinch of salt into a bowl. Rub in the butter thoroughly, and mix to a firm dough with the cold water. Chill for 15–20 minutes. Roll out on a lightly floured board and use to line the plate or ring. Chill while preparing the filling.

If low-fat soft cheese is used, first sieve it. Beat together in a bowl the cheese, sugar and cinnamon. Add the honey and mix in well. Then beat in the eggs, one at a time, beating well after each addition. Sieve the mixture, then turn it into the chilled case. Bake at 180°C, 350°F, Gas 4, for 45 minutes, then turn up the heat to 220°C, 425°F, Gas 7, and bake for another 20 minutes until the cheesecake is firm in the centre, or until a thin heated skewer run into the centre of the cake comes out clean. Turn off the heat, open the oven door and leave the cheesecake to cool in the oven. Turn out, and serve cold.

NOTE: myzithra is unsalted Greek curd cheese, sometimes available in a Greek delicatessen. Commercial skimmed milk soft cheese is quite a good substitute.

Three-Cheese Honey Cheesecake

Serves 10

Base

250 g (8 oz) wholemeal flour
2 eggs
4 tablespoons clear honey
60 g (2 oz) margarine

Filling

1×227 g (8 oz) packet Philadelphia soft cheese
125 g (4 oz) clear honey
60 g (2 oz) margarine
2 eggs, separated
2×226 g (8 oz) cartons cottage cheese
60 g (2 oz) Gruyère cheese
1 teaspoon grated nutmeg
grated rind and juice 1 lemon

Topping

Gruyère cheese to decorate

Line the base and grease the inside of a 20 cm (8 inch) loose-based cake tin. Sift the flour into a bowl, make a hollow in the centre, and put in the eggs, honey and margarine. Work them into the flour to make a soft, pasty dough. With the back of a spoon, press it evenly all over the base and sides of the tin. Chill while making the filling.

Bring the Philadelphia cheese up to room temperature. Beat together the honey, margarine and egg yolks until fully blended. Sieve in the cottage and Philadelphia cheeses, grate in the Gruyère cheese, and mix in the nutmeg, lemon rind and juice. Whisk the egg whites until fairly stiff. Stir 1 tablespoonful into the cheese mixture, then fold in the rest. Turn the mixture into the chilled case. Bake at 180°C, 350°F, Gas 4, for 50 minutes–1 hour, or until the filling is just firm and light gold. Cool in the turned-off oven with the door ajar until fully cooled, then chill for a further 12 hours at least. Before serving, grate enough cheese to make about 3 tablespoons and sprinkle over the top of the cheesecake.

Ten Minute French Cheesecake
Serves 4

Base
125 g (4 oz) puff pastry
Filling
125 g (4 oz) full-fat soft cheese
1 tablespoon clear honey
½ teaspoon vanilla essence
Topping
icing sugar

Grease a flat baking sheet, or cover with bakewell paper. Roll out the pastry on a lightly floured board into a 20 cm (8 inch) circle. Place it on the baking sheet. Bake at 220°C, 425°F, Gas 7, for 10–12 minutes. The pastry circle should have risen high, be lightly browned, and have shrunk to about 18 cm (7 inches) in diameter. Cool it on a wire rack.

While cooling, make the filling as follows. Beat the cheese until very soft, add the honey and vanilla essence, and beat until smoothly blended. Split the cooled pastry circle horizontally. Spread the filling evenly all over the bottom half. Lay the top half beside it, cut side up. Return to the oven and bake at the temperature above for 5–6 minutes, until the filling is very lightly set and the cut surface of the top half is crisp. Cool on the baking sheet; the filling will firm up as it cools. When cooled, sandwich the two halves together lightly and sprinkle the top with icing sugar. Serve with lightly whipped cream.

Honey Cheesecake
Serves 6

Base
175 g (6 oz) flour
salt
125 g (4 oz) butter
60 g (2 oz) icing sugar
1 egg yolk
1 tablespoon cold water
Filling
175 g (6 oz) full-fat soft cheese
4 tablespoons stiff honey
2 eggs
150 ml (¼ pint) double or whipping cream
¼ teaspoon grated nutmeg
Topping
15 g (½ oz) chopped walnuts
whipped cream to decorate

Sift the flour and a pinch of salt into a bowl. Rub in the butter with the fingertips until the mixture resembles breadcrumbs. Sift in the icing sugar, and stir. Beat the egg yolk with the water, add to the dry ingredients, and mix. Knead well to form a smooth dough and chill for 30 minutes. While chilling, grease a 20 cm (8 inch) flan ring on a baking sheet, and the baking sheet under it. Roll out the pastry on a lightly floured board and use to line the flan ring. Bake blind (see page 14) at 200°C, 400°F, Gas 6.

While cooling, make the filling. Mash the cheese until soft, and beat in the honey until smooth. Separately, beat the eggs, then beat them into the cheese mixture. Stir in the cream and nutmeg. Pour the mixture into the cooked case and bake at 180°C, 350°F, Gas 4, for 20 minutes until firm. Sprinkle with the nuts and bake for another 10 minutes. Cool in the flan ring and remove it when cold. Decorate with rosettes of whipped cream before serving.

Cinnamon Crumb Cheesecake
Serves 8–10

Base and Topping
175 g (6 oz) dry white breadcrumbs
90 g (3 oz) butter
60 g (2 oz) castor sugar
1½ teaspoons ground cinnamon
30 g (1 oz) chopped mixed nuts

Filling
3 eggs, separated
125 g (4 oz) castor sugar
400 g (14 oz) full-fat soft cheese
grated rind and juice 1 lemon
150 ml (¼ pint) single cream

See that the breadcrumbs are loose, fine and even. Melt the butter in a frying pan, add the breadcrumbs and turn them over with a spatula until golden. Take off the heat and stir in the sugar and cinnamon. Keep aside while you grease the sides but not the base of a 20 cm (8 inch) loose-based cake tin. Line the base with a circle of bakewell paper and press about two-thirds of the crumb mixture evenly all over it. Chill. Keep the remaining crumbs aside.

To make the filling, beat the egg yolks until liquid, adding the sugar slowly, and beating until thick and creamy. Sieve in the cheese, and work it in with a fork, blending thoroughly. Add the lemon rind, then strain and add the lemon juice, mixing thoroughly. Mix in the cream. Whisk the egg whites until they just hold soft peaks. Stir 2 tablespoons into the cheesecake mixture, then fold in the rest. Turn the mixture gently on to the chilled base. Bake at 180°C, 350°F, Gas 4, for 40 minutes or until just firm. Sprinkle the remaining crumbs and the nuts on top, and bake for a further 15 minutes. Cool in the tin. Run a sharp pointed knife round the inside of the tin to loosen the cheesecake from the sides. Remove the sides of the tin, leaving the cheesecake still on the base. Loosen the base from the tin carefully with the knife, and slide the cheesecake on to a serving plate.

Spice Cheesecake
Serves 6

Base
175 g (6 oz) flour
salt, ground cinnamon
¼ teaspoon finely grated lemon rind
90 g (3 oz) butter
30 g (1 oz) lard
1 tablespoon castor sugar
1 egg yolk
1–2 tablespoons cold water

Filling
300 g (10 oz) low-fat soft cheese
4 tablespoons double cream
175 g (6 oz) demerara sugar
½ teaspoon ground ginger
¼ teaspoon ground cinnamon
¼ teaspoon ground cloves
90 g (3 oz) pine nut kernels
2 teaspoons brandy (optional)
2 egg whites

Sift the flour, and a pinch each of salt and cinnamon into a bowl. Sprinkle with the lemon rind. Rub in the fats, and stir in the sugar. Mix the egg yolk with 1 tablespoon water, and use to bind the mixture into a smooth dough, adding the second tablespoon water if needed. Chill the pastry for 10–15 minutes. Meanwhile, grease the inside of an 18 cm (7 inch) flan case for serving. Roll out the pastry on a lightly floured board and use it to line the flan case.

To make the filling, mash the cheese until soft and mix in the cream, sugar and spices. Chop the nuts finely, add to the mixture and stir in. Mix in the brandy if used. Beat the egg whites until frothy and stir in lightly. Turn the mixture into the pastry shell. Bake at 180°C, 350°F, Gas 4, for 50 minutes–1 hour, until the cheesecake is firm in the centre. Serve warm with brown sugar and cream, or serve cold.

Dutch Brown Pie
Serves 6

Base
175 g (6 oz) flour
salt
90 g (3 oz) butter
1–2 tablespoons cold water

Filling
500 g (1 lb) full-fat soft cheese
2 tablespoons icing sugar, or to taste
ground spices to taste:
    ground cardomum, ground ginger,
    grated nutmeg, ground mace
    and ground cloves

Buy or prepare freshly-ground spices for this old sixteenth-century Dutch cheesecake, invented at the time when the Dutch were masters of Europe's spice trade. Use them as the recipe directs.

Line the base and grease the inside of a 20 cm (8 inch) loose-based sandwich layer cake tin. Sieve the flour and a pinch of salt into a bowl. Rub in the butter and mix to a firm dough with the water. Chill. Roll out on a lightly floured board and use to line the tin.

To make the filling, beat the cheese and 2 tablespoons icing sugar together until smooth. Add a good pinch each of all the spices except the cloves; use only a tiny pinch of cloves. Mix in, and taste. Then adjust the sweetness and flavourings to suit your own taste, adding enough spice to make the cheese a warm, golden-brown colour. Spoon the mixture into the pastry case, and bake at 180°C, 350°F, Gas 4, for 45 minutes. Cool in the tin. When cold, remove from the tin and serve as a spice cake, or with cream as a dessert.

Chocolate Sultana Cheesecake
Serves 6–8

Base
125 g (4 oz) flour
salt
60 g (2 oz) butter
30 g (1 oz) castor sugar
1 egg yolk
1½ teaspoons water

Filling
2 eggs
90 g (3 oz) castor sugar
250 g (8 oz) home-made, unsalted
    yogurt cheese (see page 11)
2 tablespoons single cream
grated rind and juice 1 lemon
60 g (2 oz) flour
60 g (2 oz) sultanas
90 g (3 oz) plain dark chocolate
1 egg white

Topping
30 g (1 oz) icing sugar
150 ml (¼ pint) natural yogurt
chocolate curls (see page 91)

Line the base and lightly grease the inside of a 20 cm (8 inch) loose-based cake tin. Sift the flour and a pinch of salt into a bowl. Rub in the butter with the fingertips until the mixture resembles fine crumbs. Mix in the sugar. Separately, blend the egg yolk with the water. Add to the dry ingredients and work to a smooth, firm dough. Chill for 1 hour, then roll out on a lightly floured board into a 20 cm (8 inch) round. Press the pastry round into the base of the cake tin. Chill while making the filling.

Whisk the eggs and sugar together until light and thick. Separately, beat together the cheese and cream. Strain the lemon juice, and beat it into the cheese mixture with the lemon rind. Combine lightly with the egg-sugar mixture, then fold in the flour and sultanas. Melt the chocolate in a bowl over a pan of simmering water. When melted stir into the main mixture, blending completely. Whisk the egg white until stiff and fold in gently. Turn the mixture on to the chilled pastry base, and bake at 190°C, 375°F, Gas 5, for 45 minutes–1 hour, or until the filling is just firm.

While baking, stir the icing sugar very gently into the yogurt so as not to liquify it. When the cheesecake is baked, spoon the sugar-yogurt mixture over the top. Raise the oven heat to 220°C, 425°F, Gas 7, return the cheesecake to the oven and bake for 5–10 minutes until the topping is set. Take out, and cool completely in the tin. Chill for 1–1½ hours. Decorate with chocolate curls (see page 91) just before serving.

Chocolate Marble Cheesecake
Serves 10–12

Base
250 g (8 oz) flour
40 g (1½ oz) light soft brown sugar
125 g (4 oz) butter
1 tablespoon chopped walnuts
Filling
125 g (4 oz) Polka Dots (plain
   chocolate buttons)
2½ tablespoons milk
500 g (1 lb) full-fat soft cheese
   (or use half full-fat and half low-fat
   soft cheese)
3 large eggs, separated
125 g (4 oz) castor sugar
1 teaspoon vanilla essence
Topping
40 g (1½ oz) castor sugar
1½ teaspoons vanilla essence
400 ml (¾ pint) soured cream

Grease the inside of a 30×20 cm (12×8 inch) baking tin or shallow, straight-sided dish. Mix the flour and sugar in a bowl. Cut and rub in the butter until the mixture is like crumbs. Make sure the nuts are finely chopped and stir them in. Press the mixture evenly all over the base of the tin. Bake at 180°C, 350°F, Gas 4, for 12–14 minutes until firm. Cool while making the filling.

Melt the chocolate with the milk in a small saucepan and put aside. Beat the cheese until soft and smooth. Beat in the egg yolks one at a time. Beat in the sugar and vanilla essence a little at a time. Separately, whisk the egg whites until stiff but not dry, and fold them into the cheese mixture. Spread evenly all over the cooled base and then spread the chocolate mixture very gently all over the top. Bake at 180°C, 350°F, Gas 4, for 20 minutes, or until almost set. While baking, mix the sugar and vanilla essence for the topping into the cream, blending completely. Spoon the mixture gently over the hot cheesecake, and return it to the oven for 7–8 minutes. Cool in the tin or dish, then chill for at least 12 hours before use. Cut in squares or bars for serving.

Rum Lattice Cheesecake
Serves 8

Base
125 g (4 oz) flour
30 g (1 oz) ground almonds
30 g (1 oz) castor sugar
salt
60 g (2 oz) butter
1 egg
2 tablespoons milk
Filling
60 g (2 oz) seedless raisins
1 tablespoon light rum
250 g (8 oz) low-fat soft
   cheese
40 g (1½ oz) butter
30 g (1 oz) ground almonds
60 g (2 oz) castor sugar,
   or to taste
3 eggs

Grease the inside of a 23 cm (9 inch) pie plate. Mix together the flour, almonds, sugar and a tiny pinch of salt. Rub in the butter and work in the egg. Mix to a dough with the milk. Roll out on a lightly floured board and line the pie plate, reserving the trimmings. Bake blind (see page 14) at 190°C, 375°F, Gas 5, for 8–10 minutes, or until crisp and light gold. Cool while making the filling.

Sprinkle the raisins with the rum and put aside. Beat the cheese until soft. Add the butter, almonds and sugar, and beat in. Separately, beat the eggs lightly, and put 2 tablespoons beaten egg aside. Gradually work the rest of the beaten egg into the cheese mixture. Fold in the raisins and rum. Turn the mixture into the baked pastry shell and bake at 190°C, 375°F, Gas 5, for 15 minutes. Roll out the pastry trimmings into thin strips and make a lattice pattern on top of the filling. Brush the pastry strips with the reserved egg. Return to the oven and bake for another 15 minutes, until light gold. Serve, either warm or cold, with rum-flavoured, sweetened cream.

Coffee and Rum Cheesecake

Serves 8

Base

 60 g (2 oz) margarine
 60 g (2 oz) castor sugar
 1 egg
 60 g (2 oz) self-raising flour
 $\frac{1}{2}$ teaspoon baking powder
 $\frac{1}{2}$ teaspoon grated orange rind

Filling

 90 g (3 oz) butter
 125 g (4 oz) castor sugar
 2 tablespoons instant coffee powder
 1 tablespoon boiling water
 1 tablespoon orange juice
 2 tablespoons dark rum
 1 egg
 60 g (2 oz) flour
 500 g (1 lb) full-fat soft cheese
 300 ml ($\frac{1}{2}$ pint) whipping cream

Topping

 rum-flavoured, sweetened whipped
  cream to decorate

Line the base and grease the inside of a deep 20 cm (8 inch) loose-based cake tin. Soften the margarine. Beat together all the base ingredients until smooth. Spread the mixture evenly all over the base of the tin.

Cream together the butter and sugar for the filling until light and fluffy. Dissolve the coffee powder in the water and orange juice, and add the rum. Cool to tepid, then beat into the butter-sugar mixture with the egg. Beat in the flour, a little at a time to avoid making lumps.

Separately, beat the cheese until smooth and creamy. Beat in the cream, a little at a time. Stir (do not beat) about a quarter of the cheese mixture into the coffee mixture, then stir in the rest in 2 or 3 parts. Stir well until quite smooth. Turn on to the batter base. Bake at 170°C, 325°F, Gas 3, for 1–1$\frac{1}{4}$ hours, or until the cheesecake is just firm in the middle. Cool in the turned-off oven. When quite cold, decorate the centre of the cheesecake with rosettes of rum-flavoured, sweetened whipped cream and serve.

To vary:

Coffee and Rum Crunch Cheesecake

Combine 150 g (5 oz) of gingernut or Gingerella biscuit crumbs and 60 g (2 oz) of softened butter to make a crumb base for the cheesecake instead of the batter base.

Instead of rosettes of cream, decorate the cheesecake with a star or stacked pattern of 8 brandy-snaps filled with rum-flavoured, sweetened whipped cream. Lay them on top of the cheesecake just before serving.

Coffee and Rum Cheesecake

Gelatine-set cheesecakes

Assorted Sweet and Savoury Cheesecakes

As-You-Like-It Cheesecake
Serves 4–6

Base
  125 g (4 oz) digestive biscuit crumbs
  30 g (1 oz) castor sugar
  40 g (1½ oz) butter
Filling and Topping
  grated rind and juice 1 lemon
  4 tablespoons cold water
  1 packet (15 g/½ oz) gelatine
  250 g (8 oz) full-fat soft cheese
  90 g (3 oz) castor sugar
  2 eggs, separated
  150 ml (¼ pint) soured cream
  1 tablespoon sugar

Line and grease the base of an 18 cm (7 inch) loose-based cake tin. Mix the crumbs and sugar in a bowl. Melt the butter, and mix it in. Press the mixture over the base of the tin. Chill while making the filling.

Put the lemon juice and water in a small heatproof bowl. Sprinkle on the gelatine and allow to soften. Then stand the bowl in a pan of very hot water, and stir until the gelatine dissolves. Cool to tepid. While cooling, beat the cheese until soft; beat in the castor sugar, then the egg yolks, one at a time. Stir in the cream. Stir in the gelatine slowly, to prevent lumps forming. Leave until almost set. Whisk the egg whites until stiff, and fold into the mixture. Turn it gently on to the base, and chill until set. Remove from the tin and sprinkle with the lemon rind and sugar just before serving. Top with rosettes of whipped cream if desired.

Almond and Orange Cheesecake
Serves 4–6

Base
  250 g (8 oz) almond macaroons
  90 g (3 oz) butter
  1–2 drops almond essence
Filling
  grated rind and juice 1 orange
  1 packet (15 g/½ oz) gelatine
  250 g (8 oz) low-fat soft cheese
  150 ml (¼ pint) natural yogurt
  2 tablespoons clear honey
Topping
  1 orange
  toasted flaked almonds (see page 94)

Line and lightly grease the inside of a 15 cm (6 inch) loose-based sandwich cake tin. Crush the macaroons to fine even crumbs, removing any rice paper. Melt the butter, and stir in the crumbs and essence. Press the crumbs evenly all over the base and sides of the tin. Trim the top, and brush off any loose crumbs as described on page 16. Bake for 10 minutes at 180°C, 350°F, Gas 4. Cool completely.

Put the orange juice in a small heatproof bowl. Sprinkle on the gelatine and allow to soften. Then stand the bowl in a pan of very hot water, stir until the gelatine dissolves, and put aside. Sieve the cheese into a bowl and mix in the yogurt and honey. Stir in the orange rind, and then the orange-gelatine mixture. Turn into the cooled crumb case, and chill for 3 hours or longer before use. Before serving, cut the orange flesh free of all pith, membranes and pips and cut into neat segments. Decorate the top of the cheesecake with the orange segments and nuts, and serve.

Cheddar and Honey Cheese Flan

Serves 4–6

Base
125 g (4 oz) Rich Tea biscuit crumbs
60 g (2 oz) butter or margarine
2 teaspoons clear honey

Filling
1 tablespoon sweet sherry
1 teaspoon gelatine
80 ml (3 fl oz) double cream
175 g (6 oz) mild Cheddar cheese
1 teaspoon lemon juice
60 g (2 oz) clear honey

Topping
90 g (3 oz) full-fat soft cheese
1½ teaspoons clear honey

Grease the inside of an 18 cm (7 inch) flan ring set on a flat serving plate. Make sure the crumbs are fine and even. Melt the fat and honey together gently, and stir in the crumbs. Cool slightly, and press firmly all over the base and sides of the prepared flan ring. Trim the top, and brush off any loose crumbs as described on page 16. Chill until firm.

To make the filling, put the sherry in a small, heatproof bowl. Sprinkle on the gelatine and allow to soften. Then stand the bowl in a pan of very hot water and stir until the gelatine dissolves. Cool to tepid. Whip the cream until fairly stiff. Grate the cheese finely, and fold it into the cream little by little, blending lightly but completely. Strain the lemon juice and mix with the honey, then blend with the gelatine and sherry, and stir into the cheese mixture as lightly as possible. Spread the mixture in the chilled case, and chill again until firm.

While chilling, make the topping. Beat the cheese with the honey until very soft and creamy. Just before serving, remove the flan ring, and pipe rosettes of sweetened, soft cheese on top of the cheesecake.

Savoury Gruyère Cheesecake

Serves 4–6

Base
40 g (1½ oz) butter
60 g (2 oz) plain potato crisp crumbs
30 g (1 oz) water biscuit crumbs

Filling
40 g (1½ oz) Gruyère cheese
15 g (½ oz) Parmesan cheese
300 ml (½ pint) aspic jelly
100 ml (4 fl oz) double or whipping cream
salt, cayenne pepper
2 egg whites

Topping
Gruyère cheese to decorate

Line and lightly grease the base of a 15 cm (6 inch) loose-based cake tin at least 6 cm (2¼ inches) deep. Melt the butter, work in the crumbs and press evenly all over the base of the tin. Chill while making the filling.

Grate both cheeses finely and mix. Warm the aspic jelly if solid, then cool until quite cold but not yet set. Whip the cream with a pinch of salt and pepper until it just holds soft peaks. Whisk it into the cheeses with the cold jelly. Leave in a cool place until thick and almost at setting point. While cooling, whisk the egg whites until fairly stiff. Fold them into the cheese mixture. Turn it gently on to the chilled base, and chill again until set. Grate enough Gruyère cheese to make about 1 tablespoon. Remove the cheesecake from the tin and sprinkle the cheese over the top just before serving.

Savoury Camembert Cheesecake

Savoury Camembert Cheesecake
Serves 6

Base
EITHER 1×15 cm (6 inch) shortcrust pastry
flan case
OR 40 g (1½ oz) butter
60 g (2 oz) plain potato crisp crumbs
30 g (1 oz) water biscuit crumbs
Filling
125 g (4 oz) ripe Camembert
1×113 g (4 oz) carton cottage cheese
2½ tablespoons cold water
1 packet (15 g/½ oz) gelatine
2 egg whites
150 ml (¼ pint) double cream
salt, pepper
Topping
1 tablespoon chopped chives

If making a crumb base, line and grease the base of a 15 cm (6 inch) loose-based cake tin. Melt the butter, and stir in the crumbs. Press the mixture evenly all over the base of the tin. Chill the crumb base or pastry case while making the filling.

Bring the Camembert up to room temperature and scrape or pare off the rind. Sieve both cheeses twice or process in an electric blender until smooth; do not leave any grains in the cottage cheese. Put the water in a small, heatproof bowl. Sprinkle on the gelatine and allow to soften. Then stand the bowl in a pan of very hot water and stir until the gelatine dissolves. Cool slightly. While cooling, whip the egg whites until fairly stiff. Separately, whip the cream with salt

and pepper until it just holds soft peaks.

Blend or whisk the cream lightly but thoroughly into the cheeses. Trickle in the dissolved gelatine, taking care not to let lumps of jelly form. Fold in the egg whites as lightly as possible. Turn the mixture into the pastry case or on to the crumb base, and chill again until set. Remove from the tin, and sprinkle with the chives just before serving.

Do not freeze this cheesecake.

Rich Cider Cheesecake
Serves 6–8

Base
60 g (2 oz) butter
150 g (5 oz) digestive biscuit crumbs
Filling
150 ml (¼ pint) medium-sweet cider
2 tablespoons cold water
1 packet (15 g/½ oz) gelatine
2 small eggs, separated
60 g (2 oz) castor sugar
350 g (12 oz) full-fat soft cheese
200 ml (6 fl oz) double cream

Line and grease the base of a 20 cm (8 inch) loose-based cake tin. Melt the butter and mix well with the crumbs. Press evenly all over the base of the tin. Chill while making the filling.

Bring the cider to the boil in a saucepan, and reduce to 80 ml (3 fl oz). Remove from the heat. Put the water in a small container, sprinkle on the gelatine, and allow to soften. Then add it to the hot cider and stir until it dissolves. Cool to tepid. In a large bowl, beat the egg yolks and sugar together until very pale and thick. Beat in the cheese in small portions until very smooth. Whip the cream to the same consistency as the cheese mixture and beat it in. Stir or beat in the cider and gelatine, taking care not to let lumps form. Whisk the egg whites until stiff and fold into the mixture. Turn gently on to the chilled base and chill again until set.

To serve, run a sharp knife round the inside of the cake tin, and lift out the cheesecake and base. Slide the cheesecake from the base on to a serving plate and serve with blackcurrant purée (see page 92) as a sauce.

Cheshire and Apple Cheesecake

Serves 8

Base

75 g (2½ oz) butter
250 g (8 oz) digestive biscuit crumbs
60 g (2 oz) muscovado sugar

Filling

grated rind and juice 1 large lemon
1½ packets (25 g/¾ oz) gelatine
250 g (8 oz) Farmhouse English Cheshire
    cheese (white or red)
2 eggs, separated
1½ tablespoons castor sugar
150 ml (¼ pint) soured cream
150 ml (¼ pint) double cream

Topping

2 red-skinned dessert apples
lemon juice as required or
    apple glaze (see below)

Line and grease the base of a 20–22 cm (8–8½ inch) loose-based cake tin. Melt the butter and work in the crumbs. Sieve and work in the sugar. Press the mixture evenly all over the base of the tin. Chill while making the filling.

Put the lemon juice in a small heatproof bowl, and scatter the gelatine on top. Leave to soften. Then stand the bowl in a pan of very hot water and stir until the gelatine dissolves. Leave to cool to tepid.

While cooling, finely grate or crumble the cheese. Then beat the cheese and egg yolks together until fully blended and pasty. Beat in the sugar, soured cream and lemon rind. Separately, whip the double cream until it holds soft peaks. Stir the cooled gelatine slowly into the cheese mixture, taking care not to let lumps of jelly form. Fold in the whipped cream. Whisk the egg whites to the same consistency as the mixture and fold in. Turn the mixture gently on to the chilled base, and leave in a cool place until set. Do not refrigerate. While setting, quarter and core the apples, and cut in thin, neat segments. Dip at once in lemon juice or apple glaze made as below. Drain well. Arrange in a decorative circle round the edge of the cheesecake just before serving.

Apple Glaze: Measure out 150 ml (¼ pint) bottled apple juice into a small saucepan. Put 2 level tablespoons arrowroot in a small bowl, and mix to a smooth cream with a little of the apple juice. Bring the remaining apple juice to the boil in the pan.

When boiling, remove from the heat and stir in the arrowroot cream. Return to a very low heat and simmer very gently until thick and clear, stirring once or twice slowly, round the sides of the pan only. Leave until tepid before use. Do not reheat.

Cheshire and Apple Cheesecake (Picture: Farmhouse English Cheese Information Office)

Ginger and Yogurt Cheesecake
Serves 8

Base and Topping
125 g (4 oz) gingernut crumbs
30 g (1 oz) castor sugar
60 g soft tub margarine
60 g (2 oz) crystallized ginger

Filling
200 ml (6 fl oz) cold water
2 packets (30 g/1 oz) gelatine
250 g (8 oz) low-fat soft cheese
125 g (4 oz) castor sugar
400 ml ($\frac{3}{4}$ pint) natural yogurt
ground ginger
juice 1 lemon
150 ml ($\frac{1}{4}$ pint) double cream

Line and grease the inside of a 20 cm (8 inch) loose-based cake tin. Mix the crumbs, sugar and margarine thoroughly. Press in an even layer all over the base of the tin. Chop the ginger finely and scatter 2 tablespoons over the crumb base, putting the rest aside. Chill the base while making the filling.

Put 80 ml (3 fl oz) of the water in a heatproof bowl. Sprinkle on the gelatine and allow to soften. Then stand the bowl in a pan of simmering water and stir until the gelatine dissolves. Stir in the remaining cold water and leave to cool.

Using an electric mixer if possible, beat together the cheese and sugar until smooth and soft. Beat in together the yogurt, a good pinch of ground ginger, lemon juice and cream. As soon as the gelatine mixture is cold and slightly viscous, stir it into the yogurt mixture slowly but thoroughly, taking care that no lumps form. Pour the mixture on to the chilled base, and scatter the remaining chopped ginger on top. Chill until completely set. Remove the tin. Serve with ginger and apricot sauce (see page 93) if desired.

Special Quark Cheesecake
Serves 4–6

Base
90 g (3 oz) digestive biscuit or
    gingernut crumbs
30 g (1 oz) butter

Filling
1 egg, separated
grated rind and juice 1 lemon
2 tablespoons milk
40 g ($1\frac{1}{2}$ oz) + $\frac{1}{2}$ tablespoon
    castor sugar
2 tablespoons cold water
1 tablespoon gelatine
150 ml ($\frac{1}{4}$ pint) double cream
250 g (8 oz) quark cheese

Topping
fresh or canned fruit
whipped cream to decorate

Line and grease the base of a 15 cm (6 inch) loose-based or springform cake tin. Make sure the crumbs are fine and even. Melt the butter, stir in the crumbs, and press evenly all over the base of the tin. Bake at 200°C, 400°F, Gas 6, for 5–8 minutes, until lightly browned. Cool while making the filling.

In the top of a double boiler, mix together the egg yolk, lemon rind, milk and 40 g ($1\frac{1}{2}$ oz) sugar. Stir over simmering water in the boiler until the custard thickens slightly (about 4 minutes). Remove from the heat. Put the water in a small heatproof bowl. Sprinkle on the gelatine and allow to soften. Then stand the bowl in very hot water and stir until the gelatine dissolves. Stir the mixture into the custard, add the lemon juice and leave to cool. While cooling, whisk the egg white with the remaining sugar until fairly stiff, and, separately, whip the cream until it holds soft peaks.

When the custard mixture has almost cooled, blend a little of it with the quark cheese to loosen it, then mix in the rest smoothly. Fold in the egg white, then the cream. Turn on to the baked, cooled base and chill for 4–6 hours, or overnight, until set. Remove from the tin, and decorate with fruit and rosettes of whipped cream.

Bran Flake Dessert Cheesecake
Serves 4–6

Base
    175 g (6 oz) 30% bran flakes
    90 g (3 oz) butter
    3 tablespoons clear honey

Filling
    2 eggs, separated
    60 g (2 oz) castor sugar
    250 g (8 oz) full-fat soft cheese
    4 tablespoons lemon juice
    2 tablespoons cold water
    1 packet (15 g/$\frac{1}{2}$ oz) gelatine
    150 ml ($\frac{1}{4}$ pint) double cream
    grated rind $\frac{1}{2}$ lemon

Grease the inside of a 20 cm (8 inch) flan ring on a baking sheet. Grease the baking sheet lightly too. Crush the flakes lightly between 2 sheets of paper with a rolling pin. Melt the butter and honey together in a medium-sized saucepan, and mix in the flakes thoroughly until well coated. Press the flakes firmly into the flan ring to form a shell. Trim the top, and brush off any loose crumbs as described on page 16. Bake at 180°C, 350°F, Gas 4, for 10 minutes. Cool completely.

To make the filling, cream the egg yolks and sugar together until thick and light. Beat in the cheese slowly until completely smooth. Add the lemon juice and beat until very smooth. Put the water in a small, heatproof bowl, sprinkle on the gelatine and allow to soften. Then stand the bowl in a pan of hot water and stir until the gelatine dissolves. Whip the cream until semi-stiff. Whisk the egg whites until they hold soft peaks. Mix the cream and lemon rind into the cheese mixture, then stir in the dissolved gelatine gradually to prevent lumps forming. Fold in the egg whites lightly but thoroughly, and leave to thicken. When the mixture is thickening and almost at setting point, pile it into the flan ring case. Leave in a cool place until fully set. Remove the flan ring, slide the cheesecake on to a serving plate, and serve cut in wedges.

Devonshire Cheesecake
Serves 8–10

Base
    125 g (4 oz) butter
    175 g (6 oz) digestive biscuit crumbs
    1 tablespoon castor sugar

Filling
    2 large oranges
    1 packet (15 g/$\frac{1}{2}$ oz) gelatine
    2 eggs, separated
    30 g (1 oz) castor sugar
    150 ml ($\frac{1}{4}$ pint) double or
      whipping cream
    1×226 g (8 oz) carton cottage cheese

Topping
    EITHER 8 fresh orange segments
      whipped cream to decorate
    OR hulled raspberries or strawberries
      1×113 g (4 oz) jar Devon
    clotted cream

Oil the inside of a 25 cm (10 inch) loose-based cake tin or flan ring set on a flat serving plate. (Do not use a flan case; it is difficult to serve from.) Melt the butter gently without letting it get hot. Stir in the crumbs and sugar. Press, while still hot, evenly over the base of the tin or ring. Chill until firm.

To make the filling, squeeze the juice of 1 orange into a cup, and sprinkle on the gelatine. Leave to soften. Grate the rind and squeeze the juice of the second orange, and put in a small, heavy saucepan with the egg yolks. Whisk together lightly. Then set the pan over very gentle heat, and stir or whisk until the custard has the consistency of thin lemon curd. Do not overheat or it will curdle. Remove from the heat and stir in the softened gelatine mixture; stir until the gelatine dissolves.

With a clean whisk, whisk the egg whites with the sugar until they hold soft peaks. With the same whisk, whip the cream separately until it, too, holds soft peaks. Sieve the cheese into a bowl and blend in the custard mixture lightly (or process them together briefly in an electric blender). Fold in the cream, then quickly and lightly fold in the egg whites. Turn on to the crumb base, level the top and leave to set.

When set, remove the cake tin or flan ring. Decorate the edge of the cheesecake with the orange segments and piped rosettes of whipped cream; or scatter hulled raspberries or halved strawberries on the cheesecake and serve Devon clotted cream on each helping.

Fruit-Flavoured Cheesecakes

Avocado Cheesecake
Serves 6–8

Base
40 g (1½ oz) butter
125 g (4 oz) any sweet biscuit crumbs

Filling
2½ tablespoons cold water
4 teaspoons gelatine
250 g (8 oz) low-fat soft cheese
90 g (3 oz) castor sugar
400 g (14 oz) avocado pear flesh
   (3 average pears)
2 teaspoons lemon juice
5 tablespoons whipping cream
2 egg whites

Topping
whipped cream to decorate
lemon sauce (see page 94)

Line and grease the base of an 18 cm (7 inch) loose-based cake tin. Melt the butter and work in the crumbs. Press evenly all over the base of the tin. Chill.

To make the filling, put the water in a small heat-proof bowl, sprinkle on the gelatine, and allow to soften. Then stand the bowl in a pan of very hot water and stir until the gelatine dissolves. Cool slightly. Beat the cheese with the sugar until soft and creamy. Sieve the avocado pear flesh, which should be ripe but not mushy, with the lemon juice to make it very smooth, and blend it into the cheese mixture. Stir in the gelatine. Whip the cream and whisk the egg whites separately, until fairly stiff. Then fold both into the cheese and avocado mixture. Turn on to the chilled base, and chill again until set. Remove from the tin and decorate with a few rosettes of piped cream. Serve with lemon sauce (see page 94).

This sweet, moss-coloured cheesecake has a sophisticated flavour.

Banana and Chocolate Cheesecake
Serves 8–10

Base
30 g (1 oz) milk chocolate
60 g (2 oz) butter
125 g (4 oz) milk chocolate
   digestive biscuit crumbs

Filling
4 tablespoons cold water
1 packet (15 g/½ oz) gelatine
250 g (8 oz) full-fat soft cheese
90 g (3 oz) castor sugar
2 eggs, separated
150 ml (¼ pint) natural or
   lemon-flavoured yogurt
grated rind and juice ½ lemon
150 ml (¼ pint) whipping cream
2 firm, ripe bananas

Topping
grated milk chocolate or chocolate curls
   (see page 91) to decorate

Grease the inside of a 20 cm (8 inch) loose-based cake tin. Melt the chocolate and butter on a plate over a pan of simmering water, and mix thoroughly with the crumbs. Press in an even layer all over the base of the tin. Chill while making the filling.

Put the water in a small, heatproof bowl. Sprinkle on the gelatine and allow to soften. Then stand the bowl in a pan of very hot water and stir until the gelatine dissolves. Keep aside. Beat the cheese with the sugar until soft and creamy. Beat in the egg yolks, followed by the yogurt, lemon rind and juice. Stir in the gelatine, taking care not to let lumps form. Working quickly, whip the cream until it just holds soft peaks and stir into the cheese mixture. Whisk the egg whites until fairly stiff, and fold them in. Slice the bananas, and put them in a single layer on the chilled base. Cover with the cheesecake mixture and chill until set. Remove the tin, and decorate the top with grated chocolate or chocolate curls before serving.

Do not freeze this cheesecake.

Blackcurrant Skim Cheesecake

Serves 4–6

Base
30 g (1 oz) butter
1 tablespoon golden syrup
150 g (5 oz) digestive biscuit crumbs

Filling
3 eggs, separated
300 ml ($\frac{1}{2}$ pint) skimmed milk, or
    dried skimmed milk
    powder made up with water
30 g (1 oz) castor sugar
2 tablespoons cold water
1 packet (15 g/$\frac{1}{2}$ oz) gelatine
250 g (8 oz) cream cheese or
    full-fat soft cheese
$\frac{1}{2}$ teaspoon grated lemon rind
1 tablespoon lemon juice

Topping
250 g (8 oz) fresh blackcurrants
4 tablespoons+2 teaspoons cold water
30 g (1 oz) castor sugar
2 teaspoons arrowroot

Line and grease the inside of a loose-based 15 cm (6 inch) square, or an 18 cm (7 inch) round cake tin. Melt the butter and syrup together gently. Cool slightly. Mix the crumbs with the butter and syrup. Press evenly all over the base of the cake tin. Chill while making the filling.

Whisk the egg yolks with a fork until liquid. Mix with the skimmed milk in a saucepan, and heat gently, stirring continuously, until the custard thickens. Remove from the heat and stir in the sugar. Leave to cool. Whisk the egg whites until stiff and put aside. Put the water in a small heatproof bowl. Sprinkle on the gelatine and allow to soften. Then stand the bowl in a pan of very hot water, and stir until the gelatine dissolves. Mash the cheese with a fork to soften it, gradually trickling in the gelatine, custard and the lemon rind. Strain the lemon juice and mix in. Whisk the mixture until it begins to thicken; then fold in the whisked egg whites lightly. Spoon the mixture over the chilled crumb base and leave in a cool place to set.

To make the topping first top and tail the blackcurrants. Then put them in a saucepan with the 4 tablespoons water and sugar. Bring gently to the boil, and cook for 2 minutes. Strain the juice into a clean pan and keep the fruit aside. Blend the arrowroot to a cream with the 2 tablespoons cold water and stir into the juice. Heat gently, stirring, until the mixture clears and thickens. Add the fruit. Cool, covered.

Remove the cheesecake from the tin and peel off the lining paper. Place on a serving dish and spoon the blackcurrant sauce over. Serve at once, with whipped cream.

White Grape Cheesecake

Serves 8

Base and Topping
60 g (2 oz) butter
175 g (6 oz) Lincoln or similar
    sweet biscuit crumbs
1×439 g (15$\frac{1}{2}$ oz) can white sultana
    grapes in syrup

Filling
150 ml ($\frac{1}{4}$ pint) natural grape juice
1$\frac{3}{4}$ teaspoons gelatine
250 g (8 oz) full-fat soft cheese
30 g (1 oz) castor sugar
225 ml (7 fl oz) whipping cream

Put the grape juice for the filling in a small heatproof bowl, sprinkle on the gelatine and allow to soften. Then stand the bowl in a pan of very hot water and stir until the gelatine dissolves. Leave the bowl in a cool place to chill until the jelly is just beginning to thicken. Meanwhile, prepare the base and cheese mixture while cooling.

For the base, line and grease the base of a 20 cm (8 inch) loose-based cake tin. Melt the butter, mix well with 150 g (5 oz) of the crumbs, putting the rest aside. Press the mixture evenly all over the base of the tin and chill. Drain the can of grapes thoroughly, and lay the fruit in an even layer on the chilled crumb crust.

Mash the cheese until soft, sprinkle in the sugar, and pour in the cream. Beat together until completely blended, smooth and thick. As soon as the jelly begins to thicken, beat or stir it into the cheese mixture without letting lumps of jelly form. Spoon at once on to the prepared base, level the top and chill until set. Remove from the tin and sprinkle the reserved crumbs on top, before serving.

Cherry Charlotte Cheesecake

Serves 4–6

Base

2 tablespoons red cherry jam
24 boudoir or sponge
   finger biscuits

Filling

250 g (8 oz) fresh or canned morello
   cherries
water as required
lemon juice as required
clear honey as required
1 packet (15 g/$\frac{1}{2}$ oz) gelatine
250 g (8 oz) low-fat soft cheese
150 ml ($\frac{1}{4}$ pint) soured cream
2 egg whites

Topping

whipped cream and red cherry jam
   to decorate

Using bakewell paper, line the base and sides of a 15 cm (6 inch) loose-based or springform cake tin. Sieve the jam. Place biscuits round the sides of the tin, set on end, with the sugared or rounded sides outward. Use the jam to stick the long edges of the biscuits together so that there are no gaps between them. Trim the projecting tops of the biscuits level with the rim of the tin. Keep the trimmed-off pieces and remaining whole biscuits aside.

If fresh fruit is used, first remove the stalks. Then simmer the cherries in a very little water, a few drops of lemon juice if required, and honey to taste, until they are soft. Remove the stones and drain, reserving the syrup. If canned cherries are used, simmer them in their own syrup with the same flavourings. Stone if necessary and drain, reserving the syrup. Allow the fruit to cool.

Place 3 tablespoons of the reserved syrup in a small heatproof bowl. Sprinkle on the gelatine and allow to soften. Then stand the bowl in a pan of very hot water, and stir until the gelatine dissolves. Cool until tepid. While cooling, beat the cheese until soft and creamy, and mix in the cream. Separately, whisk the egg whites until stiff but not dry.

Mix the cooled gelatine into the cheese-cream mixture, stirring well to prevent any lumps forming. Chill until just beginning to thicken. Fold in the fruit, then the egg whites. Spoon the mixture gently into the sponge biscuit case, and level the top. Cover with a flat layer of the reserved biscuits and biscuit pieces. Chill for 2–3 hours.

Invert the tin on to a serving plate. Remove the tin, and gently peel off the bakewell paper. Decorate the top of the cheesecake with alternate rosettes of piped whipped cream and blobs of red jam.

Loganberry Cheesecake

Serves 6

Base

60 g (2 oz) butter
125 g (4 oz) any plain biscuit crumbs

Filling and Topping

1 × 410 g (14$\frac{1}{2}$ oz) can loganberries in syrup
1 packet (15 g/$\frac{1}{2}$ oz) gelatine
125 g (4 oz) full-fat soft cheese
4 tablespoons dried skimmed milk powder
   made up to 300 ml ($\frac{1}{2}$ pint) with water
1 tablespoon lemon juice
1 tablespoon kirsch
60 g (2 oz) castor sugar
5 tablespoons whipping cream
1 teaspoon arrowroot
$\frac{1}{2}$ teaspoon extra kirsch (optional)

Line and grease the base of an 18 cm (7 inch) loose-based cake tin. Soften the butter and mix with the crumbs thoroughly. Press evenly all over the base of the tin. Chill while making the filling.

Drain the fruit reserving 12 loganberries for the topping, and the syrup. Sieve the rest of the fruit to make a smooth purée. Put 2 tablespoons of the reserved syrup in a small heatproof bowl, sprinkle on the gelatine and allow to soften. Stand the bowl in a pan of very hot water and stir until the gelatine dissolves. Cool to tepid.

Soften the cheese and mix smoothly with the milk. Mix in the lemon juice, kirsch, and sugar. Stir in the loganberry purée lightly. Whip and fold in the cream. Mix in the gelatine slowly but thoroughly, without letting lumps form. Turn the mixture on to the chilled base, level the top and chill again until set.

To make the topping, measure out 150 ml ($\frac{1}{4}$ pint) of the reserved syrup. Blend a little of the measured quantity with the arrowroot to make a smooth cream. Bring the rest to the boil in a small saucepan. Blend in the arrowroot cream, and simmer until the syrup thickens and clears. Remove the pan from the heat and gently mix in the reserved fruit and the extra kirsch if used. Cool, covered. When ready to serve, remove the cheesecake from the tin, and spoon the cooled syrup over it.

Strawberry Cottage Cheesecake
Serves 6–8

Base
75 g (2½ oz) butter
250 g (8 oz) digestive biscuit crumbs

Filling
3 eggs, separated
juice 1 lemon
6 tablespoons cold water
2 packets (30 g/1 oz) gelatine
175 g (6 oz) castor sugar
salt
250 ml (8 fl oz) milk
grated rind 2 lemons
1×226 g (8 oz) carton cottage cheese
250 g (8 oz) full-fat soft cheese
150 ml (¼ pint) double cream

Topping
250 g (8 oz) fresh strawberries
icing sugar

Line and grease the base of a 20 cm (8 inch) loose-based cake tin. Melt the butter, and mix in the crumbs. Press evenly all over the base of the tin. Chill.

To make the filling, beat the egg yolks until liquid and strain the lemon juice. Put the water in a small heatproof bowl, sprinkle on the gelatine and allow to soften. Then add the sugar and a pinch of salt. In a medium-sized saucepan, heat the gelatine mixture very gently until the gelatine dissolves and the sugar melts. Stir in the egg yolks and the milk, and continue stirring until the mixture is almost on the boil, and the custard thickens. Remove from the heat, and stir in the lemon juice and rind. Cool. While cooling, sieve the cottage cheese and beat it with the soft cheese until creamy. When the gelatine mixture is tepid, mix it into the cheeses lightly with the cream. Whisk the egg whites until fairly stiff, and fold them in. Pile the mixture on the crumb base, and chill until firm. Decorate with the strawberries and sprinkle lightly with icing sugar just before serving.

Longley Pineapple Cheesecake
Serves 8

Base
90 g (3 oz) digestive biscuit crumbs
1 tablespoon castor sugar
40 g (1½ oz) butter

Filling and Topping
2×226 g (8 oz) cartons cottage cheese
1×219 g (7¾ oz) can pineapple rings in syrup
1 packet (15 g/½ oz) gelatine
grated rind and juice 1 lemon
125 g (4 oz) castor sugar
2 eggs, separated
150 ml (¼ pint) double cream
sprigs fresh mint

This cheesecake is prepared upside down and inverted just before serving. Oil the base of a 20 cm (8 inch) loose-based cake tin. Sieve the cottage cheese. Drain the can of pineapple over a heatproof basin, sprinkle the gelatine into the syrup, and allow to soften. Reserve 1 pineapple ring for topping the cheesecake; cut it into neat segments and put aside. Chop the rest of the fruit very finely and mix with the cheese, lemon rind and juice.

Stand the basin containing the pineapple syrup in a pan of very hot water, and stir until the gelatine dissolves. Blend together the sugar and egg yolks, and add them to the gelatine mixture. Stir over very low heat until the custard is the consistency of pouring cream. Cool. While cooling, whip the cream and whisk the egg whites until stiff but not dry. When the custard is thick but not yet set, blend it into the cheese mixture, then fold in the egg whites and cream. Turn the mixture into the prepared tin, and leave to set.

See that the crumbs for the base are fine and even. Combine them with the sugar, then melt and work in the butter to make a crumbly mixture. Sprinkle the mixture over the set cheesecake, and press down lightly. Leave to firm up. Run a sharp-pointed knife round the edge of the crust, and invert the cheesecake on to a 25 cm (10 inch) serving plate. Remove the tin and decorate with the reserved pineapple pieces and with mint sprigs.

Lemon and Redcurrant Cheesecake (Picture: Kellogg Company of Great Britain Ltd.)

Lemon and Redcurrant Cheesecake
Serves 6–8

Base
90 g (3 oz) butter
3 tablespoons golden syrup
175 g (6 oz) 30% bran flake crumbs

Filling
2 eggs, separated
60 g (2 oz) castor sugar
250 g (8 oz) full-fat soft cheese
3 tablespoons lemon juice
2 tablespoons cold water
1 packet (15 g/$\frac{1}{2}$ oz) gelatine
150 ml ($\frac{1}{4}$ pint) double or whipping cream

Topping
4 tablespoons redcurrant jelly
2 tablespoons warm water
125 g (4 oz) fresh redcurrants and castor
sugar as required (optional)

All the ingredients should be at room temperature. Line and grease the base and sides of a 22 cm (8$\frac{1}{2}$ inch) loose-based sandwich cake tin. Melt the butter and syrup together in a medium-sized saucepan, and stir in the crumbs until well coated all over. Press the crumbs over the base and sides of the tin to form a shell. Trim the top and brush off any loose crumbs as described on page 16. Bake for 10 minutes at 180°C, 350°F, Gas 4. Remove from the oven and cool completely.

Cream the egg yolks and sugar thoroughly. Sieve the cheese and beat it in slowly, until very smooth. Trickle in the lemon juice, and beat until fully blended in. Put the water in a small heatproof bowl, sprinkle on the gelatine and allow to soften. Then stand the bowl in a pan of very hot water, and stir until the gelatine dissolves. Cool to tepid. Whip the cream until semi-stiff, and whisk the egg whites until they form soft peaks. Mix the tepid gelatine into the cheese mixture thoroughly. When it thickens and is almost at setting point, fold in the cream and then the egg whites quickly and lightly, blending completely in each case. Turn the mixture into the cooled shell, and smooth the top level. Leave until fully set.

To make the topping, melt the redcurrant jelly with the water, and leave until almost cold but not yet reset. If you wish, add sweetened fresh redcurrants to the topping. Spoon it lightly over the filling and leave to set. Run a sharp knife round the inside of the tin to loosen the case. Remove the cheesecake, and slide it on to a serving plate. Serve cut in wedges.

Fresh Raspberry Cheesecake

Fresh Raspberry Cheesecake
Serves 8–10

Base
90 g (3 oz) butter
250 g (8 oz) sweetened oatcake
 biscuit crumbs

Filling
2 tablespoons cold water
1 packet (15 g/½ oz) gelatine
grated rind and juice 1 lemon
350 g (12 oz) low-fat soft cheese
90 g (3 oz) castor sugar
2 eggs, separated
300 ml (½ pint) double cream
2 teaspoons kirsch

Topping
500 g (1 lb) fresh raspberries

Grease the inside of a 23 cm (9 inch) loose-based cake tin. Melt the butter, and mix with the crumbs. Press the mixture in an even layer all over the base of the tin. Bake at 180°C, 350°F, Gas 4, for 8 minutes. Cool while making the filling.

Put the water in a small heatproof bowl, sprinkle on the gelatine and allow to soften. Then stand the bowl in a pan of very hot water and stir until the gelatine dissolves. Cool to tepid. Strain the lemon juice and mix the lemon rind and juice into the gelatine mixture.

Beat the cheese with the sugar until soft and creamy. Beat in the egg yolks, one at a time, until the mixture is light and fluffy. Beat the gelatine and lemon mixture into the cheese mixture, taking care not to let lumps of gelatine form. Whip the cream with the kirsch until it just holds soft peaks, and fold into the cheese mixture. Whisk the egg whites until fairly stiff, and fold them in. Turn gently on to the baked base and chill until set.

Hull the raspberries. Remove the cake tin and arrange the fruit on top of the cheesecake just before serving.

Cheesecakes Set with Flavoured Jelly

Cottage Custard Cheesecake
Serves 10

Base
   1×30 cm (12 inch) bought sponge flan case

Filling and Topping
   lemon jelly tablet to set
      600 ml (1 pint) liquid
   5 tablespoons boiling water
   1 egg
   2 egg yolks
   40 g (1½ oz) castor sugar
   5 tablespoons milk
   1×226 g (8 oz) carton cottage cheese
   grated rind and juice 1 lemon
   ½ teaspoon vanilla essence
   2 egg whites
   200 ml (7 fl oz) whipping cream

Chop the jelly tablet. Pour the boiling water over the chopped jelly and stir until dissolved. Mix together in a heatproof basin the egg, egg yolks, sugar and milk. Place the basin over a pan of simmering water, and stir until the custard thickens. Strain into a clean basin, stir in the dissolved jelly thoroughly, and leave to cool. While cooling, sieve the cheese. When the custard begins to thicken at the edges, mix in the cheese, lemon rind and juice, and vanilla essence. Beat the egg whites until they hold soft peaks. Stir two tablespoons into the cheese mixture, then fold in the rest. Whip the cream lightly. Fold rather more than half of it into the filling mixture. Turn gently into the sponge case, and chill until set. Decorate with the remaining cream, piped in rosettes.

Do not freeze this cheesecake.

Highland Cheesecake
Serves 4

Base
   40 g (1½ oz) butter
   90 g (3 oz) plain oatcake crumbs
   30 g (1 oz) dark soft brown sugar

Filling and Topping
   orange jelly tablet to set
      600 ml (1 pint) liquid
   Drambuie liqueur to taste (optional)
   150 ml (¼ pint) boiling water
   2 tablespoons orange jelly marmalade
   250 g (8 oz) full-fat soft cheese
   60 g (2 oz) castor sugar
   grated rind 1 orange
   150 ml (¼ pint) orange juice
   golden oatmeal topping (see page 91)

Line and grease the base of a 15 cm (6 inch) loose-based cake tin. Melt the butter, and mix in the crumbs and sugar. Press the mixture evenly all over the base of the tin. Chill while making the filling.

Put half the jelly tablet aside. Chop the remaining ½ jelly tablet. Substitute 1–2 tablespoons Drambuie for an equal quantity of boiling water if you wish. Pour the hot liquid over the chopped jelly, and stir until dissolved. Leave to cool until beginning to thicken. While cooling, spread the marmalade thinly over the chilled base. Beat the cheese until soft, and beat in the sugar and orange rind.

When the jelly is approaching setting point, mix it lightly, little by little, into the cheese, taking care not to let lumps form. Turn the mixture on to the chilled base, and chill again until set.

Put the reserved ½ jelly tablet in a heatproof bowl, and make jelly for the topping with the orange juice in the same way as for the filling mixture, substituting 1–2 tablespoons Drambuie for an equal quantity of orange juice if you wish. Cool. Just before it reaches setting point, pour a few spoonfuls at a time over the filling, and rotate the tin to spread the jelly evenly. Chill for at least 30 minutes. Remove from the tin and sprinkle with one third the recipe quantity of golden oatmeal topping (see page 91) just before serving.

Pineapple Jelly Cheesecake
Serves 8

Base
60 g (2 oz) butter
125 g (4 oz) Butter Osborne crumbs
30 g (1 oz) castor sugar
1×376 g (13¼ oz) can crushed pineapple
    in natural juice

Filling
½ pineapple jelly tablet to set
    300 ml (½ pint) liquid
150 ml (¼ pint) natural pineapple
    juice from can
cold water as required
250 g (8 oz) full-fat soft cheese
225 ml (7 fl oz) whipping cream
1 tablespoon castor sugar (optional)

Topping
½ pineapple jelly tablet to set
    300 ml (½ pint) liquid
slightly less than 150 ml (¼ pint) cold water

Make the jellies for the filling and topping before the base to give them chance to set.

To make the filling, chop the ½ jelly tablet and put in a small, heatproof bowl. Drain the juice from the can crushed pineapple (see base ingredients), making up to 150 ml (¼ pint) with water if necessary. Add the juice to the chopped jelly and allow to soften. Then stand the bowl in a pan of very hot water and stir until the jelly dissolves. Leave the bowl in a cool place, or chill, until beginning to set. Meanwhile prepare the jelly for the topping in exactly the same way, but using a little less water than usual, to make a stiff jelly. Leave in a cool place to set firmly,

For the base, line and grease the base of a 20 cm (8 inch) loose-based cake tin. Melt the butter and mix thoroughly with the crumbs and sugar. Press the mixture evenly all over the base of the tin and chill. Drain the pineapple well and spread over the base.

For the filling, mash the cheese until soft. Add the cream, and beat or whisk together until completely blended, smooth and thick. Add the sugar while whisking if you wish to sweeten the filling mixture. As soon as the jelly for the filling begins to thicken, beat or stir it into the cheese mixture thoroughly, without letting lumps of jelly form. Spoon at once on to the prepared base, level the top and chill until set. While chilling, chop the jelly for the topping.

Remove the cheesecake from the tin when set and cold, and decorate with the chopped jelly.

Apple and Walnut Cheesecake
(Picture page 60)
Serves 8–10

Base
125 g (4 oz) gingernut crumbs
30 g (1 oz) light soft brown sugar
60 g (2 oz) soft tub margarine
30 g (1 oz) finely chopped walnuts

Filling
lemon jelly tablet to set
    600 ml (1 pint) liquid
1 packet (15 g/½ oz) gelatine
200 ml (6 fl oz) boiling water
1×410 g (14½ oz) can unsweetened
    evaporated milk
1×227 g (8 oz) packet Philadelphia soft cheese
125 g (4 oz) castor sugar
400 ml (¾ pint) sweetened, smooth apple sauce,
    home-made or canned
1 teaspoon vanilla essence
1 teaspoon lemon juice

Topping
5 walnut halves
30 g (1 oz) finely chopped walnuts

Start making the filling before the base. Chop the jelly tablet. Add the unflavoured gelatine to the chopped jelly and pour the boiling water over both. Stir until dissolved, then leave to cool. Chill the evaporated milk and bring the cheese up to room temperature.

Meanwhile make the base. Line the base and grease the inside of a 20 cm (8 inch) springform cake tin. Mix the crumbs, sugar and margarine thoroughly. Add the nuts for the base and press evenly all over the base and about 2.5 cm (1 inch) of the sides of the cake tin. Chill.

Using an electric mixer if possible, beat together the cheese and sugar for the filling until smooth and creamy, gradually adding the apple sauce, vanilla essence and lemon juice. As soon as the gelatine mixture begins to thicken, beat it in. Then beat in the chilled evaporated milk, and continue beating at high speed until the mixture is thick and light. Pour into the chilled case, and decorate with the walnut halves and chopped nuts. Chill for at least 4 hours or overnight before use.

Apple and Walnut Cheesecake (page 59)

Summer Orange Cheesecake
Serves 12

Base
200 g (7 oz) butter
350 g (12 oz) Rich Tea or similar
    biscuit crumbs
125 g (4 oz) castor sugar

Filling
4 large oranges
¾ lemon jelly tablet to set
    400 ml (¾ pint) liquid
150 ml (¼ pint) very hot water
500 g (1 lb) full-fat soft cheese
125 g (4 oz) castor sugar

Topping
¼ lemon jelly tablet to set
    150 ml (¼ pint) liquid
4 tablespoons very hot water
juice 1 orange
3 oranges
1×227 g (8 oz) jar fine shred
    orange marmalade

Lightly grease the inside of a 25 cm (10 inch) flan
ring and place it on a flat serving plate. Soften the
butter and work the crumbs and sugar into it until
well blended. Press the mixture evenly all over the
base and sides of the flan ring. Trim the top and
brush off any loose crumbs as described on page
16. Chill.

To make the filling grate the rind from 1 of the
oranges, and squeeze the juice of all 4. Chop the ¾
jelly tablet and put it in a basin with the water. Stir
until the jelly dissolves, then add the orange juice and
cool to tepid. Beat the cheese until soft with the sugar
and orange rind. Trickle in the tepid jelly, beating all
the time to prevent lumps forming. Spoon the filling
into the chilled case, and chill again until set.

While chilling, make the topping. Chop the ¼ jelly
tablet and put it in a basin with the water. Stir until
dissolved. Add the orange juice, and chill until firmly
set. Cut the flesh of the oranges for decorating free of
all skin, pith and pips. Arrange the segments of flesh
around the edge of the cheesecake. Warm the marmalade just enough to make it liquid, brush it over
the cheesecake and chill. Chop the clear orange jelly
and heap it in the centre of the cheesecake. Remove
the flan ring and serve.

Summer Orange Cheesecake (Picture: Summer Orange Office)

Tangy Jelly Cheesecake

Serves 4

Base

40 g (1½ oz) butter
90 g (3 oz) rolled oats
30 g (1 oz) light soft brown sugar
1 teaspoon ground cinnamon

Filling

½ orange jelly tablet to set
   300 ml (½ pint) liquid
150 ml (¼ pint) boiling water
2 tablespoons orange jelly marmalade
250 g (8 oz) low-fat soft cheese
60 g (2 oz) castor sugar
grated rind 1 orange

Topping

½ orange jelly tablet to set
   300 ml (½ pint) liquid
juice 1 orange
boiling water as required

Line the base and grease the inside of a 15 cm (6 inch) loose-based cake tin. Melt the butter, and stir in the oats, sugar and cinnamon. Mix well adding a little more melted butter if necessary. Press the mixture evenly all over the base of the tin. Chill while making the filling.

Chop the ½ jelly tablet, put in a heatproof bowl and pour the water over. Stir until the jelly has dissolved. Leave to cool for 30 minutes or until almost cold and just beginning to thicken. While cooling, spread the marmalade thinly over the chilled base. Beat the cheese until soft and beat in the sugar and orange rind.

When the jelly is almost at setting point, mix it lightly, a few spoonfuls at a time, into the cheese mixture. Do not let lumps of jelly form. Turn the mixture on to the chilled base, cover loosely and chill again until set.

Make a jelly for the topping in the same way, using the ½ jelly tablet and orange juice made up to 150 ml (¼ pint) with boiling water. Stir until the jelly dissolves. Cool. Just before it reaches setting point, pour a few spoonfuls over the chilled cheesecake, leaving any remaining jelly to set. Tilt and rotate the tin to spread it evenly over the surface before it sets. Chill for at least 30 minutes. Chop any remaining jelly and arrange round the edge of the cheesecake. Then remove the tin and serve.

Lime Cheesecake

Serves 8

Base

60 g (2 oz) gingernut crumbs
60 g (2 oz) Butter Osborne biscuit crumbs
2 tablespoons castor sugar
60 g (2 oz) soft tub margarine

Filling

lime jelly tablet to set
   600 ml (1 pint) liquid
1 packet (15 g/½ oz) gelatine
200 ml (6 fl oz) undiluted, sweetened lime juice
250 g (8 oz) low-fat soft cheese
125 g (4 oz) castor sugar
300 ml (½ pint) natural yogurt
1×410 g (14½ oz) can unsweetened
   evaporated milk
4 tablespoons double or whipping cream
3–4 drops green food colouring

Topping

30 g (1 oz) angelica

Line the base and grease the inside of a 23 cm (9 inch) loose-based or springform cake tin. Mix the crumbs, sugar and margarine thoroughly. Press evenly all over the base of the tin.

Chop the jelly tablet. Add the unflavoured gelatine to the chopped jelly in a small saucepan, and pour the lime juice over. Heat gently, stirring, until the jelly and gelatine dissolve. Cool.

Using an electric mixer if possible, beat together the cheese and sugar for the filling until smooth and soft. Beat in the yogurt, then the evaporated milk and cream. As soon as the jelly mixture is cold and viscous, stir it in slowly and thoroughly, without letting lumps of jelly form. Stir in the food colouring. Pour the mixture on to the chilled base. Chill until set, them remove the tin. Finely chop the angelica and scatter it over the top. Serve with single cream.

Party Cheesecakes

Apricot Jam Cheesecake
Serves 8

Base
> 60 g (2 oz) butter
> 175 g (6 oz) shortbread biscuit crumbs
> grated rind 1 orange
> 40 g (1½ oz) castor sugar

Filling
> 300 ml (½ pint) water
> 1½ packets (25 g/¾ oz) gelatine
> juice 1 orange
> 6 tablespoons smooth apricot jam
> 500 g (1 lb) low-fat soft cheese
> 5 tablespoons whipping cream

Topping
> canned apricot halves or
>   apricot jam to decorate

Using bakewell paper, line and grease the base of a 20 cm (8 inch) loose-based cake tin. Do not fit the sides on to the base for the moment. Soften the butter and work in the crumbs, 1 teaspoon orange rind and sugar. Press the mixture all over the base of the tin, leaving the edge clear. Put on a baking sheet and bake for 8 minutes at 180°C, 350°F, Gas 4. Cool. Fit the sides on the tin.

Put the water in a small heatproof bowl. Sprinkle on the gelatine and allow to soften. Stand the container in a pan of very hot water, and stir until the gelatine dissolves. Add the remaining orange rind, and strain and add the orange juice. Cool or chill until quite cold but not yet set.

Spread 2 tablespoons jam over the cooled baked base, then beat the rest into the cheese until blended. Beat in the gelatine mixture gradually, taking care not to let lumps of jelly form. Whip the cream and fold in evenly. Turn the mixture on to the prepared base, and chill until set. Remove the cheesecake from the tin. Before serving place a ring of canned apricot halves (well-drained), or spoon a ring of apricot jam round the edge of the cheesecake.

Nesselrode Cheesecake
Serves 4–6

Base
> 75 g (2½ oz) butter
> 150 g (5 oz) Marie biscuit crumbs

Filling and Topping
> 90 g (3 oz) glacé cherries
> 60 g (2 oz) chopped mixed peel
> 250 g (8 oz) full-fat soft cheese
> 2 tablespoons clear honey
> 175 g (6 oz) unsweetened, canned
>   chestnut purée
> 200 ml (6 fl oz) whipping cream
> 1 tablespoon light rum
> 2 tablespoons cold water
> 1 packet (15 g/½ oz) gelatine

Make the base. Line and grease the base of a deep 15 cm (6 inch) loose-based cake tin. Melt the butter and stir in the crumbs. Press them evenly over the base of the prepared tin. Chill.

Put 3 glacé cherries aside for decoration. Rinse the rest in hot water, pat dry and chop finely. Mix with the peel and put aside.

Sieve the cheese and mix in the honey, blending thoroughly. Sieve the chestnut purée if stiff. Whip the cream until semi-stiff, and mix it with the chestnut purée and rum until smooth and well blended. Fold the cheese and chestnut mixtures together. Put the water in a small heatproof bowl, sprinkle on the gelatine and allow to soften. Then stand the bowl in a pan of very hot water and stir until the gelatine dissolves. Allow to cool. Stir into the cheese mixture gradually to prevent lumps forming. Chill the mixture until thick and almost at setting point.

Assemble the dessert as follows. Spoon an even layer of cheese mixture over the chilled base. Sprinkle well with cherry-peel mixture. Working quickly, repeat layers until both mixtures are used, finishing with a layer of cheese mixture. Smooth the top level or make a swirled pattern as desired. Cover loosely, and chill until fully set and firm, then remove the tin. Halve the remaining cherries and use to decorate before serving.

The chestnut and peel flavours are intriguing, but may not appeal to everyone at first.

Ginger and Rum Freezer Cheesecake

Ginger and Rum Freezer Cheesecake

Serves 8–10

Base
1 bought Jamaica ginger cake

Filling
500 g (1 lb) full-fat soft cheese
100 g (3½ oz) castor sugar
3 eggs, separated
4 teaspoons light rum
30 g (1 oz) crystallized ginger
grated rind 1 orange
2 tablespoons cold water
1 packet (15 g/½ oz) gelatine
350 ml (12 fl oz) whipped dessert
   topping made with 150 ml (¼ pint) milk

Topping
6–8 brandy-snaps

Line and grease the base of a 23 cm (9 inch) loose-based cake tin. Cut the cake into even-sized slices and cover the base of the tin with them. Press down well.

Beat the cheese and sugar together until smooth. Beat in the egg yolks one at a time and stir in the rum.

Finely chop the ginger and mix in with the orange rind. Put the water in a small heatproof bowl, sprinkle on the gelatine, and allow to soften. Then stand the bowl in a pan of very hot water and stir until the gelatine dissolves. Stir it gently but thoroughly into the cheese mixture. Stir in the made-up dessert topping lightly. Quickly whisk the egg whites to the same consistency as the cheese mixture and fold them in. Turn the mixture on to the cake base, and chill until firm. Remove from the tin to serve.

Just before serving, crush the brandy-snaps and scatter them over the cheesecake. Alternatively, leave the brandy-snaps whole and arrange them in a star pattern on the cheesecake

If you wish to freeze the cheesecake, do so before it is decorated. Freeze it uncovered until firm, then wrap and freeze for storage. Thaw for 4 hours at room temperature before decorating and serving.

Garibaldi Cheesecake

Garibaldi Cheesecake
Serves 10

Base
90 g (3 oz) plain chocolate
75 g (2½ oz) butter
275 g (9 oz) digestive biscuit crumbs
Filling
3×85 g (3 oz) packets Philadelphia
   soft cheese
100 g (3½ oz) castor sugar
1 packet (15 g/½ oz) gelatine
¼ teaspoon salt
2 eggs, separated
150 ml (6 fl oz) milk
1 teaspoon vanilla essence
250 ml (8 fl oz) whipping cream
30 g (1 oz) ground almonds
2–3 drops almond essence
2–4 drops green food colouring

Line and grease the base of a 20 cm (8 inch) square pan about 5 cm (2 inches) deep. Melt the chocolate and butter for the base, mix with the crumbs, and press evenly all over the base of the tin. Chill while making the filling.

Bring the cheese up to room temperature and beat until soft. Mix 60 g (2 oz) of sugar, the gelatine and salt in a fairly large saucepan. Beat the egg yolks lightly in the milk, and add to the pan. Mix well, then stir over medium heat until the mixture is just on the boil. Remove from the heat at once. Beat the cheese into the hot mixture little by little. Cool until barely warm.

Beat the egg whites with the vanilla essence until they hold soft peaks. Continue beating, adding the remaining sugar gradually, until the meringue is stiff and glossy. Mix 2 tablespoons into the cheese mixture to loosen it, then fold in the rest, leaving no lumps. Whip the cream separately until it just holds soft peaks and fold it in likewise.

Divide the mixture in half. Stir lightly into one half the almonds, almond essence and enough colouring to tint the mixture green. Spread it evenly on the chilled base. Gently, spoon the uncoloured half on top. Chill for at least 6 hours, then cut in slices or bars for serving.

Black Forest Cheesecake

Serves 8–10

Base

90 g (3 oz) plain chocolate
75 g (2½ oz) butter
275 g (9 oz) plain chocolate digestive
   biscuit crumbs

Filling and Topping

1 × 425 g (15 oz) can pitted black cherries
   in syrup
350 g (12 oz) full-fat soft cheese
90 g (3 oz) castor sugar
2 eggs, separated
1 tablespoon kirsch
2 tablespoons cold water
1 packet (15 g/½ oz) gelatine
300 ml (½ pint) double cream
1 tablespoon arrowroot
kirsch or lemon juice to taste
chocolate curls (see page 91)

Line and grease the base of a 23 cm (9 inch) loose-based cake tin. Melt the chocolate and butter for the base together and mix with the crumbs. Press the mixture evenly all over the base of the tin and chill.

Drain the cherries, reserving the syrup, and cut them in half. Spread about one-third of the fruit on the chilled base and keep the rest aside. Cream the cheese and sugar together thoroughly, then beat in the egg yolks and kirsch. Put the water in a small heatproof bowl, sprinkle on the gelatine and allow to soften. Then stand the bowl in a pan of very hot water and stir until the gelatine dissolves. Leave to cool slightly while you beat the cream until it just holds soft peaks, and whisk the egg whites until stiff. Beat the gelatine into the cheese mixture little by little, taking care not to let lumps form, then fold in the cream, and finally the egg whites. Turn gently on to the base and chill until firm.

Make a cherry sauce. Blend the arrowroot to a cream with a little of the reserved syrup. Put the rest in a pan, add kirsch or lemon juice to taste, and bring just to boiling point. Stir in the arrowroot cream and continue stirring until the liquid thickens and clears. Use hot, or cool under damped paper for use cold.

Remove the tin from the cheesecake. Just before serving, decorate the top with the remaining cherries. Spoon a little cherry sauce over the cherries, and arrange the chocolate curls around the edge. Serve the remaining cherry sauce separately.

The cheesecake can be frozen before decoration.

Whipped Cream Cheesecake

Serves 8

Base

100 g (3½ oz) butter
250 g (8 oz) Butter Osborne or similar
   biscuit crumbs
60 g (2 oz) castor sugar

Filling

125 g (4 oz) castor sugar
6 tablespoons cold water
¼ teaspoon salt
2 packets (30 g/1 oz) gelatine
2 eggs, separated
175 ml (6 fl oz) unsweetened evaporated milk
1 teaspoon grated lemon rind
350 g (12 oz) full-fat soft cheese
juice 2 small lemons
1½ teaspoons vanilla essence
100 ml (4 fl oz) whipping cream

Topping

100 ml (4 fl oz) whipping cream
3 tablespoons blanched almonds

Line the base and grease the inside of a 20 cm (8 inch) loose-based cake tin. Melt the butter without letting it get hot, and work in the crumbs and sugar. Press the mixture evenly all over the base of the tin. Chill while making the filling.

Mix together 90 g (3 oz) of the sugar, the water and salt in a medium-sized saucepan. Sprinkle on the gelatine and allow to soften. Then heat gently, stirring, until the gelatine and sugar melt. Stir in the egg yolks quickly, then the evaporated milk. Continue stirring over very gentle heat until the mixture thickens. Remove from the heat, add the lemon rind and leave to cool. While cooling, sieve the cheese and mix into it the lemon juice and vanilla essence. Whisk the egg whites until stiff, gradually adding the remaining sugar. Separately, whip the cream until it holds soft peaks.

When the custard mixture is tepid, stir in the cheese mixture gently until thoroughly blended; it should thicken at once. Fold in the egg whites and cream, lightly but thoroughly. Turn the mixture gently on to the base, and chill until set.

Whip the cream for the topping and crush the nuts. Before serving decorate with the cream and scatter the nuts on top. Serve cold.

Chocolate and Lemon Curl Cheesecake

Serves 6

Base

125 g (4 oz) butter
2 tablespoons clear honey
200 g (7 oz) digestive biscuit crumbs
60 g (2 oz) plain chocolate

Filling

250 g (8 oz) full-fat soft cheese
juice ½ lemon
1 egg, separated
2 tablespoons clear honey
150 ml (¼ pint) cold milk
vanilla essence
2 teaspoons brandy (optional)
2 tablespoons cold water
1 packet (15 g/½ oz) gelatine

Topping

½ lemon
30 g (1 oz) plain chocolate

Line the base and grease the inside of a 20 cm (8 inch) loose-based sandwich cake tin, or a flan ring set on a baking sheet. Melt the butter and honey for the base, and work in the crumbs. Press the mixture evenly all over the base and sides of the tin or ring. Trim the top, and brush off any loose crumbs as described on page 16. Break up the chocolate for the base, and melt it on a plate over a pan of simmering water. Spread it evenly all over the base of the case. Chill while making the filling.

Soften the cheese well with the back of a spoon, working in the lemon juice. Separately, beat the egg yolk, honey and milk together in a heatproof bowl until blended. Stand the bowl in a pan of simmering water, and beat until the custard thickens. Cool for 2 minutes, then beat it into the cheese little by little, with a few drops of vanilla essence and the brandy if used. Put the water in another heatproof bowl, sprinkle on the gelatine and allow to soften. Then stand the bowl in a pan of very hot water and stir until the gelatine dissolves. Cool for 2–3 minutes, then stir lightly but thoroughly into the cheese mixture, taking care not to let lumps of jelly form. Leave until almost at setting point.

Whisk the egg white until it holds soft peaks, and fold into the cheese mixture. Turn the mixture quickly into the chilled case, and chill again until set.

While setting, slice the ½ lemon. Then cut each slice from the centre to the edge, and twist it to form a curl. Melt the chocolate for the topping on a plate over a pan of simmering water. Just before serving, arrange the lemon curls on the cheesecake, and pipe on lines of chocolate to decorate it.

Mocha Cheesecake

Serves 8

Base

75 g (2½ oz) butter
60 g (2 oz) milk chocolate
30 g (1 oz) castor sugar
125 g (4 oz) milk chocolate digestive
   biscuit crumbs

Filling

1 tablespoon cocoa powder
300 ml (½ pint) cold black coffee
1½ packets (25 g/¾ oz) gelatine
500 g (1 lb) full-fat soft cheese
125 g (4 oz) castor sugar
5 tablespoons–150 ml (¼ pint) whipping cream

Topping

milk chocolate and milk chocolate
   curls or caraque (see page 91) to decorate

Line and grease the base of a 20 cm (8 inch) loose-based cake tin. Soften the butter and melt the chocolate on a plate over a pan of simmering water. Work the chocolate into the butter with the sugar and crumbs. Press the mixture evenly all over the base of the tin.

Mix the cocoa powder to a smooth cream with a little of the coffee. Put the rest of the coffee in a heatproof bowl, sprinkle on the gelatine and allow to soften. Blend in the cocoa cream, then stand the bowl in a pan of very hot water and stir until the gelatine dissolves. Cool to tepid. While cooling, beat the cheese and sugar together until creamy. Trickle in the cooled gelatine mixture, beating all the time to prevent lumps of jelly forming. Whip the cream separately and whisk into the cheese mixture. Turn on to the chilled base, and chill again until set.

While chilling grate enough chocolate to make 2–3 tablespoons, and make chocolate curls as described on page 91. When the cheesecake is set remove from the tin. Decorate the sides with grated chocolate and the top with chocolate curls or caraque before serving.

Other unbaked cheesecakes and flans

Hollywood Cheese Flan
Serves 6–8

Base
1×18 cm (7 inch) pastry tart or flan shell,
baked blind, (see page 14)

Filling
EITHER 250–300 g (8–10 oz) fresh fruit
OR 1×397 g (14 oz) can fruit (see note below)
castor sugar to taste (optional)
1–2 teaspoons sweet liqueur (optional)
1×226 g (8 oz) carton cottage cheese
4 tablespoons natural yogurt
1½–2 tablespoons clear honey
single cream (optional)

Cool the pastry shell if newly baked. If using canned fruit, drain it well. Slice the fruit, canned or fresh, and spread it in a flat layer all over the base. Sprinkle fruit with sugar if tart, and with 1–2 teaspoons suitable liqueur, if desired. Sieve the cottage cheese into a bowl. Stir in the yogurt gently, with honey to taste depending on the sharpness of the yogurt. Chill for 30 minutes to let the yogurt firm up. Spoon the mixture over the fruit in the shell. Chill for another 6–8 hours, or overnight if possible. Serve with single cream if desired.

NOTE: fresh cultivated blackberries, raspberries, strawberries or sliced bananas, sprinkled with lemon juice, are all good fruits to use. Well-drained canned peaches, apricots or pineapple, sprinkled with lemon juice, can be used instead of fresh fruit if necessary. For a liqueur, sprinkle soft fruit with kirsch, bananas or pineapple with rum, and peaches or apricots with Grand Marnier.

Coconut-Orange Cheesecake
Serves 4

Base
250 g (8 oz) coconut macaroons
90 g (3 oz) butter

Filling
250 g (8 oz) low-fat soft cheese
150 ml (¼ pint) natural yogurt
2 tablespoons clear honey
grated rind 1 orange

Topping
5 crystallized orange slices
2 tablespoons desiccated coconut

Line and grease the inside of a 15 cm (6 inch) loose-based sandwich cake tin. Crush the macaroons to fine even crumbs, removing any rice paper. Melt the butter and mix with the crumbs. Press the mixture evenly over the base and sides of the tin. Trim the top and brush off any loose crumbs as described on page 16. Chill until firm.

Sieve the cheese and mix with the yogurt, honey and orange rind. Spoon into the chilled case, and refrigerate for 6–8 hours before use. To serve, remove from the tin and decorate with the crystallized orange slices and desiccated coconut.

Cheddar and Almond Cheesecake (Picture: Dairy Produce Advisory Service of the Milk Marketing Board)

Cheddar and Almond Cheesecake
Serves 6–8

Base
30 g (1 oz) light soft brown sugar
2 teaspoons golden syrup
100 g (3½ oz) butter
175 g (6 oz) digestive biscuit crumbs

Filling and Topping
60 g (2 oz) flaked almonds
80 ml (3 fl oz) double cream
175 g (6 oz) Cheddar cheese
1 teaspoon lemon juice
60 g (2 oz) castor sugar

Put an 18 cm (7 inch) flan ring on a baking sheet. Line and grease the inside of the ring. Melt the sugar, syrup and butter and stir in the crumbs. Press the mixture evenly all over the base of the flan ring. Chill while making the filling.

Toast 30 g (1 oz) of the nuts (see page 94), chop them and put aside. Whip the cream lightly. Grate the cheese and fold or stir into the cream with the lemon juice and sugar. Sprinkle the chilled base with the remaining, untoasted nuts, then spread the cheese mixture on top. Sprinkle the top with the toasted nuts. Leave in a cool place until firm. Remove the flan ring, and serve.

Almond and Sherry Cheese Torte
Serves 6

12 boudoir or sponge finger biscuits
2½ tablespoons cold water
4 teaspoons gelatine
2 egg whites
250 g (8 oz) low-fat soft cheese
100 g (3½ oz) castor sugar
150 ml (¼ pint) double cream
6 drops almond essence, or to taste
5 tablespoons sweet sherry
toasted flaked almonds to decorate
  (optional, see page 94)

Crush 4 biscuits to fine even crumbs. Cut the ends off the rest so that they fit in a radiating or star pattern in an 18 cm (7 inch) cake tin. Keep them aside with the cut ends. Grease the inside of the cake tin generously with butter, and coat with the crumbs. Reserve any crumbs left over. Put the water in a small heat-proof bowl, sprinkle on the gelatine and allow to soften. Then stand the bowl in a pan of very hot water and stir until the gelatine dissolves. Cool to tepid.

While cooling, beat the egg whites until fairly stiff. In a separate bowl, beat the cheese with the sugar until soft and creamy. Whip the cream until fairly stiff, and blend it into the cheese mixture with the almond essence. Trickle and beat in the dissolved gelatine, taking care not to let lumps of jelly form. Taste and adjust the flavouring if desired. Fold in the egg whites as lightly as possible. Turn half the mixture into the tin and spread evenly. Dip the cut biscuits in the sherry, and arrange in a star pattern on the mixture. Fit in the cut ends between them to cover the surface. Spread the remaining cheese mixture on top. Chill until set. Remove from the tin, and decorate with any reserved crumbs or with the nuts just before serving.

Creamy Pear Cheesecake
Serves 8

Base
- 100 g (3½ oz) butter or margarine
- 250 g (8 oz) Gingerella biscuit crumbs

Filling
- juice 2 lemons
- water as required
- 60 g (2 oz) castor sugar, or as required
- 2 eggs, separated
- 2 packets (30 g/1 oz) gelatine
- 750 g (1½ lb) full-fat or low-fat unsalted soft cheese (see note below)
- 2 cooked or canned pears
- 300 ml (½ pint) double or whipping cream
- 2 teaspoons grated lemon rind
- 60–90 g (2–3 oz) chopped mixed nuts

Line and grease the base of a 20 cm (8 inch) loose-based cake tin. Melt the fat without letting it get hot. Mix with the crumbs and press the mixture evenly all over the base of the tin. Chill while making the filling.

Make the lemon juice up to 150 ml (¼ pint) with water. Put 60 g (2 oz) of sugar, the egg yolks, gelatine, lemon juice and water in a heatproof basin. Stand the basin in a pan of simmering water and stir until the gelatine dissolves. Do not let the egg set round the sides of the basin. Remove from the heat and allow to cool. Meanwhile, separately sieve the cheese, drain and sieve the pears and whip the cream. When the gelatine mixture is almost cold, blend in the cheese, pears, cream and lemon rind. Taste and add extra sugar if desired. Whisk the egg whites to the same consistency as the cheese mixture and fold them in lightly. Spoon the mixture over the chilled base, and chill until set. Then remove the cheesecake from the tin and press the nuts gently on the sides before serving.

NOTE: unsalted soft cheese is available in health food stores if you do not make your own.

Low-Fat Fruit Cheesecake
Serves 4–6

Base and Topping
- 75 g (2½ oz) low-fat margarine-style spread
- 125 g (4 oz) water biscuit crumbs
- 1×198 g (7 oz) can low-calorie fruit salad

Filling
- 1×226 g (8 oz) carton cottage cheese
- 150 ml (¼ pint) natural yogurt
- 1½ tablespoons clear honey or
  - 2 tablespoons syrup from can of fruit
- grated rind 1 lemon and ½ orange

Bring the spread to room temperature and mix with the crumbs. Line with bakewell paper the inside of an 18 cm (7 inch) loose-based sandwich cake tin or pie plate. Press the crumbs evenly all over the base and sides. Trim the top, and brush off any loose crumbs as described on page 16. Chill for 1 hour. While chilling, drain the fruit salad thoroughly, reserving the syrup.

Sieve the cheese, and gently mix in the yogurt, honey or syrup, and rind. Spoon into the chilled case and refrigerate for 6–8 hours. Remove from the tin and pile the drained fruit on top just before serving.

Plum Pie Cheesecake
Serves 4–6

Base
- 1×18 cm (7 inch) pastry flan case, baked blind, (see page 14)

Filling
- 200 g (7 oz) plum pie filling (about ½×383 g (14½ oz) can)
- 250 g (8 oz) full-fat soft cheese
- 150 ml (6 fl oz) double cream
- 1 teaspoon lemon juice
- 30 g (1 oz) castor sugar

Use the pastry of your choice for the flan case. Sieve the pie filling. Put the cheese and cream into a bowl, and beat them together until thick and smooth. Beat in the lemon juice and sugar. Then beat in 2–3 tablespoons pie filling. Taste, and add any extra pie filling needed to give the flavour and consistency you want, putting the remaining pie filling aside. Beat again until the mixture is smooth, then pile it into the flan case. Chill well. Spoon pie filling round the edge of the cheesecake to decorate.

Easter Holiday Cheese Gâteau
Serves 4–6

1 round sponge or light fruit cake about
   15 cm (6 inches) across and
   7.5 cm (3 inches) high
2×226 g (8 oz) cartons cottage cheese
125 g (4 oz) castor sugar
1 tablespoon double cream
salt, ground cinnamon
2 tablespoons sweet sherry
2 teaspoons lemon juice
60 g (2 oz) chopped mixed peel
250 g (8 oz) marzipan
apricot glaze as required (see page 93)
small sugar Easter eggs to decorate (optional)

Make sure the top of the cake is flat and level. Split it horizontally into four equally thick layers. Put the bottom layer into a deep loose-based or springform cake tin into which it fits snugly.

Sieve the cheese into a mixing bowl with the sugar. Add the cream, a pinch each of salt and cinnamon, the sherry and lemon juice, and mix until well blended. Fold in the peel. Spread one third of the mixture evenly over the cake layer in the tin. Cover with a second cake layer, and spread evenly with cheese mixture. Repeat the process, then cover with top cake layer. Place a circle of greaseproof paper and a light weight on top, and leave in a cool place overnight.

Roll out 125 g (4 oz) of the marzipan into a thin strip which will cover the sides of the gâteau. Heat the apricot glaze gently and spread it lightly over the sides of the cake. Wrap the marzipan strip round the gâteau, joining the ends with a little extra glaze. Paint the top of the gâteau with glaze. Roll the remaining marzipan into 11 small balls and attach them, at equal intervals, around the rim with dabs of extra glaze if needed. Decorate the centre of the top of the gâteau with sugar eggs if desired.

Sicilian Cheese Gâteau
Serves 4

1 round sponge cake about 15 cm (6 inches)
   across and 7.5 cm (3 inches) high
500 g (1 lb) ricotta cheese or
   2×226 g (8 oz) cartons cottage cheese
125 g (4 oz) castor sugar
1 tablespoon double cream
40 g (1½ oz) bitter-sweet chocolate
   (optional)
salt
3 tablespoons Marsala wine
60 g (2 oz) toasted flaked almonds
   (see page 94)
175–250 g (6–8 oz) marzipan, tinted green
apricot glaze as required
   (see page 93)
white glacé icing flavoured with a few drops
   almond essence and lemon juice

Split the cake horizontally into four equally thick layers. Put the bottom layer in a deep loose-based or springform cake tin into which it fits snugly.

Sieve the cheese into a mixing bowl with the sugar. Mix in the cream. Grate the chocolate coarsely if used, and stir most of it into the cheese with a pinch of salt and the wine; reserve enough grated chocolate to decorate the top of the gâteau. Chop the nuts roughly and fold into the mixture. Spread one third of the mixture evenly over the cake layer in the tin. Cover with a second cake layer, and spread evenly with cheese mixture. Repeat the process, then cover with the top cake layer. Place a circle of greaseproof paper and a light weight on top, leave in a cool place overnight, and then remove from the tin.

Roll out the marzipan into a strip which will cover the sides of the gâteau. Warm the glaze and spread it lightly over the sides of the cake. Wrap the marzipan round the gâteau joining the ends with a little glaze. Cover the top with glacé icing. When almost firm, decorate with the reserved chocolate, if used.

Cassata Cheesecake

Cassata Cheesecake
Serves 10

Cake Layers
3 eggs, separated
40 g (1½ oz) castor sugar
2 teaspoons orange juice
1 teaspoon grated orange rind
salt
30 g (1 oz) flour

Filling
750 g (1½ lb) low-fat soft cheese
75 g (2½ oz) castor sugar
100 ml (4 fl oz) double cream
60 g (2 oz) glacé fruits (cherries, pineapple, etc)
60 g (2 oz) plain chocolate (optional)

Covering
300 ml (½ pint) whipping cream
60 g (2 oz) icing sugar
glacé fruit to decorate (optional)

Line and grease the base and sides of a 33×23 cm (13×9 inch) Swiss roll tin. Beat together the egg yolks and sugar until thick and pale. Beat in the orange juice and rind. Separately, whisk the egg whites and a pinch of salt until stiff. Fold a quarter of the egg whites into the yolk mixture, then pour the yolk mixture over the remaining whites, and sprinkle with the flour. Fold the mixtures together until fully blended. Turn into the tin, level with a spatula, and bake at 180°C, 350°F, Gas 4, for 15 minutes, or until lightly browned. Invert on to greaseproof paper, cool and peel off the backing sheet.

For the filling, beat the cheese until soft with the sugar and cream. Divide into two equal portions. Chop the fruit, grate the chocolate if used, and fold both into 1 portion.

Line the base of a 20×10×7 cm (8×4×3 inch) loaf tin. Cut a piece of the cake to fit the base of the tin. Cover it evenly with the plain cheese mixture. Cut a second piece of the cake and fit into the loaf tin. Spoon over it the cheese and fruit mixture. Level the top. Trim the remaining cake to fit the top of the tin. Lay it on the mixture, and cover with greaseproof paper. Place a light weight on top, and chill overnight.

Whip the cream for the covering, adding the icing sugar while whipping. Remove the cheesecake from the tin by inverting it on to a serving plate. Cover it smoothly with most of the cream, using a palette knife or spatula for spreading. Pipe the remaining cream in whorls or rosettes. Chop the fruit and use to decorate the cheesecake if desired.

To vary:
Liqueured Party Cheesecake

Make as above but add 4 tablespoons Grand Marnier to the cheese mixture without fruit, and 4 tablespoons of the same liqueur to the whipped cream covering.

Pashka

Although pashka is not, strictly, a cheesecake, so many people have asked for it that a traditional and a modern version have been included here. In the past, the Russian Orthodox Church made Easter a glorious eating celebration, and pashka was its crowning centrepiece. Shaped like a pyramid in an eight-sided wooden mould, it was served with a tall cylindrical fruit loaf, called a kulich, and was left on the Easter buffet table for a week after the festival, for all comers. To keep it moist, the pashka stood covered with a damp napkin, and kept well in the still-cold climate. Even the simpler, modern version will keep for several days if stored in the refrigerator or a cool place.

Either version of pashka can be made in a large, clean flower pot. The cheese will be cylindrical instead of pyramidal, but it does not matter. Alternatively, the cheese can be moulded and drained in cottage cheese cartons with holes pierced in the bottom; this may well be more practical for modern use in small families, since the dessert is a rich one. Cartons not used at once can be foil-wrapped and stored for 2 weeks in the refrigerator, or make good Easter gifts for friends.

Traditional Pashka

Makes about 1 kg (2 lb) or
  8×113 g (4 oz) cartons cheese

600 g (1¼ lb) dry, home-made milk
  curd cheese (see page 11),
  or use dry, low-fat soft cheese
  without preservatives
3 eggs, separated
250 g (8 oz) sugar
½ teaspoon vanilla essence
150 ml (¼ pint) soured cream
125 g (4 oz) butter
125 g (4 oz) blanched almonds
2–3 tablespoons chopped mixed peel
40 g (1½ oz) seedless raisins

Crumble the cheese and sieve it twice. Separately, beat the egg yolks, adding the sugar gradually, until pale and fluffy. Stir in the vanilla essence and cream. Melt the butter and slowly add to the egg-sugar mixture. Beat until fully blended, then mix lightly but thoroughly with the cheese. Turn into a heavy-based saucepan. Beat the egg whites until stiff, and fold or blend in. Shred the nuts and fold in with the peel and raisins.

Cook very gently in a double boiler, stirring occasionally with a fork, just until bubbles form at the edge of the pan. Cool in the pan.

Use a large flower pot with holes in the bottom, or pierce holes in cottage cheese cartons. Line the pot or cartons with dampened, thin cotton or butter muslin. Fill with the cooled cheese mixture. Tap the pot or cartons once or twice on the table-top while filling to knock out any airholes. Place the pot or cartons on a tray or in a baking tin to drain. After 6–8 hours, lay a circle of greaseproof paper on top of the pot or each carton, and weight it lightly. Leave in a cool place overnight or for 24 hours.

Next day, peel off the paper and turn out the cheese on to a dish, if for use at once, or refrigerate for storage. If left at room temperature, keep covered with a napkin or handkerchief wrung out in cold water.

Modern Pashka

Makes about 1 kg (2 lb) or
  8×113 g (4 oz) cartons cheese

500 g (1 lb) full-fat soft cheese
250 g (8 oz) butter
250 g (8 oz) castor sugar
4 egg yolks
vanilla essence to taste
500 g (1 lb) mixed dried and glacé fruits and nuts
  (sultanas, glacé pineapple, glacé cherries,
  angelica, flaked almonds)

Sieve the cheese and soften the butter. In a warmed bowl, cream the butter, sugar and egg yolks together until the sugar dissolves and all three ingredients are well blended. Add vanilla essence to taste, then blend in the cheese. Wash and dry any glacé fruit thoroughly, and chop it. Then fold the dried and glacé fruit and nuts into the cheese mixture. Line a pot or cartons as in the previous recipe, and fill with the cheese. Weight, drain, and use or store like traditional pashka.

NOTE: when making either traditional or modern pashka use a 1 kg (2 lb) weight for a large pot of cheese, a 175 g (6 oz) weight for a carton.

Soft Lemon Cheesecake

Serves 6

Base
  1×19 cm (7½ inch) pastry shell, baked blind,
    (see page 14)
Filling
  3×85 g (3 oz) packets Philadelphia soft cheese
  100 ml (4 fl oz) lemon juice,
    fresh or bottled
  3 eggs
  125 g (4 oz) castor sugar
  ½ teaspoon vanilla essence
Topping
  2 teaspoons grated lemon rind

Use the pastry of your choice. The pastry shell should be well cooled if newly baked.

Bring the cheese up to room temperature and strain the lemon juice. Mash the cheese well with a fork. Beat the eggs in a heatproof basin until thick and fluffy, gradually adding the sugar, lemon juice and vanilla essence. Place the basin over a pan of simmering water. Stirring constantly, cook until the custard is very thick; do not let clots form. Beat the cheese into the hot custard, blending thoroughly until smooth. Let the mixture cool completely. Spoon into the pastry shell, and chill well before use. Sprinkle with freshly grated lemon rind just before serving.

To vary:
Soft Lemon and Apple Cheese Flan

Use 80 ml (3 fl oz) bottled apple juice and 2 tablespoons strained lemon juice instead of lemon juice only. Make as above.

Soft Orange Cheese Flan

Use 80 ml (3 fl oz) strained orange juice and 2 tablespoons strained lemon juice instead of lemon juice only. Use freshly grated orange and lemon rind, mixed, to decorate.

Buckinghamshire Cherry Cheesecake

Serves 8

Base
  125 g (4 oz) butter
  200 g (7 oz) digestive biscuit crumbs
Filling
  1×397 g (14 oz) can sweetened
    condensed milk
  1×226 g (8 oz) carton cottage cheese
  150 ml (¼ pint) double cream
  4 tablespoons lemon juice
Topping
  EITHER 500 g (1 lb) fresh black cherries
    150 ml (¼ pint) water
    30 g (1 oz) castor sugar
  OR 1×425 g (15 oz) can pitted black
    cherries in syrup
  1 tablespoon arrowroot
  1 teaspoon gelatine

Oil the inside of a 23 cm (9 inch) flan case or pie plate. Melt the butter, remove from the heat, and stir in the crumbs. Press the mixture evenly all over the base and sides of the case or plate. Chill for 1 hour.

Tip the condensed milk into a bowl, sieve in the cheese and beat well. Whip the cream until it just holds soft peaks. Stir the lemon juice into the cheese mixture, then fold in the cream. Turn the mixture into the chilled case and refrigerate overnight.

Stalk and pit fresh cherries if used, and cook with the water and sugar until tender. Drain, reserving the syrup, and cool. Drain canned cherries, reserving the syrup. Blend 2 tablespoons cherry syrup with the arrowroot and gelatine to make a smooth cream. Heat the rest of the syrup to boiling point, and stir in the arrowroot and gelatine mixture. Boil for 1 minute, cover the pan and remove from the heat. Cool. Arrange the cherries on the cheesecake, and spoon the thickened syrup over them. Chill at the lowest temperature in the refrigerator for 1 hour before serving from the dish.

Low-cost cheesecakes

Cottage Orange Cheesecake
Serves 4–6

Base
- 90 g (3 oz) butter or margarine
- 250 g (8 oz) water biscuit crumbs

Filling and Topping
- 2 eggs, separated
- 60 g (2 oz) castor sugar
- 1½ packets (25 g/¾ oz) gelatine
- 300 ml (½ pint) unsweetened orange juice
- 2×226 g (8 oz) cartons cottage cheese
- 1 orange

Grease the inside of an 18 cm (7 inch) loose-based sandwich cake tin, about 5 cm (2 inches) deep. Melt the fat and stir in the crumbs. Press the crumb mixture evenly over the base and sides. Trim the top and brush off any loose crumbs as described on page 16. Chill the case, to firm it up.

Put the egg yolks, sugar, gelatine and orange juice in a heatproof basin. When the gelatine softens, stand the basin in a pan of simmering water, and stir until the gelatine dissolves. Do not let the egg set at the edges of the basin. Put the basin in a cool place, to cool down. While it cools, sieve the cheese, and grate the rind of the orange. As soon as the gelatine mixture is 'gummy' at the edges, stir it into the cheese lightly, with the grated rind. Whisk the egg whites until fairly stiff. Stir 2 tablespoons into the cheese mixture, then fold in the rest as lightly as possible. Pour the mixture gently into the chilled crumb crust and chill again until set.

Divide the orange into segments, freed of pith, membranes and pips. When the cheesecake is set, remove from the tin and decorate with the orange segments before serving.

Cottage Supper Cheesecake
Serves 4–6

Base
- 175 g (6 oz) shortcrust pastry

Filling
- 60 g (2 oz) butter
- 200 g (7 oz) cottage cheese
- 1 egg
- salt, grated nutmeg
- 125 g (4 oz) castor sugar
- 30 g (1 oz) currants
- 1 tablespoon flour
- 1 teaspoon baking powder

Grease the inside of an 18 cm (7 inch) flan case, or flan ring on a baking sheet. Roll out the pastry on a lightly floured board and use to line the case or ring. Chill while making the filling.

Melt the butter without letting it get hot. Sieve the cheese. Beat the egg into the cheese thoroughly, blending completely, then mix in the butter, a pinch of salt, the sugar, currants and a pinch of grated nutmeg. Sprinkle with the flour and baking powder, and stir them in. Turn the mixture into the chilled pastry case. Bake at 190°C, 375°F, Gas 5, for 25 minutes or until the filling is risen and lightly browned. Cool in the turned-off oven with the door ajar for 20 minutes, then remove the flan ring if used, and leave in a cool place until firm. Serve while just still warm, or cold.

Do not freeze this cheesecake.

Curd and Currant Cheese Flan

Serves 4–6

Base

175 g (6 oz) puff pastry

Filling

60 g (2 oz) hard block margarine
150 g (5 oz) low-fat soft cheese
60 g (2 oz) full-fat soft cheese
1 egg
salt, ground mixed spice
125 g (4 oz) castor sugar
30 g (1 oz) currants
1 tablespoon flour
1 teaspoon baking powder

Grease the inside of a 19 cm (7½ inch) flan ring set on a lined baking sheet. Roll out the pastry on a lightly floured board and use to line the ring. Chill while making the filling.

Melt the margarine without letting it get hot. Beat the cheeses together until well blended and creamy. Beat in the egg, margarine, a pinch of salt, the sugar, currants and a pinch of the spice. Sprinkle with the flour and baking powder, and stir them in. Turn the mixture into the chilled case. Bake at 190°C, 375°F, Gas 5, for 25 minutes or until the filling is risen and lightly browned. Cool for 20–30 minutes in the turned-off oven with the door ajar, then remove the flan ring and finish cooling on the sheet at room temperature. Serve the same day.

Do not freeze this cheesecake.

North Country Curd Tart

Serves 6–8

Base

175 g (6 oz) shortcrust pastry

Filling

350 g (12 oz) home-made milk curd cheese, (see page 11), or cottage cheese
60 g (2 oz) castor sugar
2 eggs
40 g (1½ oz) currants (optional)
30 g (1 oz) sultanas (optional)
grated nutmeg

Grease the inside of an 18 cm (7 inch) pie plate. Roll out the pastry on a lightly floured board and use to line the plate. Sieve the cheese and stir in the sugar. Beat the eggs lightly and blend them in, then add the fruit if desired. Turn the mixture into the pastry shell, and sprinkle with nutmeg. Bake at 190°C, 375°F, Gas 5, for 20–25 minutes until just set in the centre and lightly browned. Serve warm or cold from the plate the same day.

Do not freeze this cheesecake.

Yorkshire Cottage Cheesecake or Tart

Serves 6

Base

125 g (4 oz) butter
30 g (1 oz) lard
200 g (7 oz) flour
2–3 tablespoons cold water

Filling

1×226 g (8 oz) carton cottage cheese
60 g (2 oz) butter
1 egg
150 ml (¼ pint) milk
40 g (1½ oz) castor sugar
2 tablespoons seeded raisins
grated rind ½ lemon

Grease a deep 20 cm (8 inch) flan ring set on a heavy baking sheet. Grease the baking sheet inside the ring as well. Make pastry by rubbing the fats into the flour until the mixture resembles breadcrumbs. Mix to a smooth dough with the water. Roll out the pastry on a lightly floured board, and line the ring with it. Chill while making the filling.

Sieve the cottage cheese and melt the butter. Beat the egg in the milk until liquid, then beat into the cheese with the sugar. Beat until smooth. (Alternatively, process all the ingredients briefly in an electric blender.) Stir in the melted butter, raisins and lemon rind. Turn themixture into the pastry case. Bake at 190°C, 375°F, Gas 5, for 30 minutes or until the pastry is cooked and the filling is just set. Serve warm or cold.

Budget Cheese Pie

Serves 4

Base

    125 g (4 oz) water biscuit crumbs
    40 g (1½ oz) soft tub margarine

Filling

    250 g (8 oz) low-fat soft cheese
    1 egg, separated
    4 tablespoons double cream
    grated rind ½ orange or lemon
    30 g (1 oz) castor sugar
    15 g (½ oz) sultanas (optional)

Topping

    1 thin slice fresh orange or lemon
      without rind

Line the base and grease the inside of a 15 cm (6 inch) pie plate. Work the crumbs into the margarine. Press the mixture evenly all over the base of the plate. Chill while making the filling.

Mix together all the filling ingredients except the egg white. When smoothly blended, whisk the egg white until stiff, and fold it in. Turn on to the chilled base and bake at 190°C, 375°F, Gas 5, for 30–35 minutes or until the filling is set. Cool in the turned-off oven with the door ajar.

To decorate, cut the fresh fruit slice from the centre to the edge, and twist it into a curled shape. Lay it in the centre of the cheesecake and serve from the plate.

Salzburg Curd Cake

Makes 12 cheesecake fingers

Base

    2 tablespoons Marie biscuit crumbs

Filling

    60 g (2 oz) butter
    90 g (3 oz) castor sugar
    2 eggs
    ½ teaspoon vanilla essence
    250 g (8 oz) low-fat soft cheese
    60 g (2 oz) self-raising flour
    1 tablespoon milk
    30 g (1 oz) sultanas

Topping

    icing sugar

Line the base and grease the inside of a shallow baking tin about 25×15 cm (10×6 inches) in size.

Dust the inside well with crumbs. Cream together the butter and sugar until soft and light. Beat in the eggs, one at a time, then the vanilla essence. Sieve and beat in the cheese with the flour and milk. Stir in the sultanas. Turn the mixture into the tin in an even layer, and bake at 190°C, 375°F, Gas 5, for 45 minutes or until firm and lightly browned. Leave at room temperature for 30 minutes until the cheesecake has shrunk slightly from the sides of the tin. When completely cold, dust the top of the cheesecake with icing sugar and cut into fingers for serving.

Lemon and Spice Cheesecake

Serves 6

Base and Topping

    150 g (5 oz) Gingerella biscuit crumbs
    ¼ teaspoon ground mixed spice
    60 g (2 oz) butter

Filling

    350 g (12 oz) full-fat soft cheese
    75 g (2½ oz) castor sugar
    2 eggs
    juice ½ lemon
    1×198 g (7 oz) can sweetened
      condensed milk
    2 tablespoons self-raising flour

Line the base and grease the inside of a 20 cm (8 inch) loose-based sandwich cake tin about 5 cm (2 inches) deep. Mix 2 tablespoons crumbs with the spice and put aside. Melt the butter and mix in the rest of the crumbs. Press the mixture evenly all over the base and 1 cm (½ inch) of the sides of the tin. Chill.

Put all the ingredients for the filling in a bowl, and beat, using an electric beater if possible, until smooth and fully blended. Pour into the chilled case, and sprinkle with the reserved crumb mixture. Bake at 180°C, 350°F, Gas 4, for 55 minutes–1 hour. Run a sharp, pointed knife round the inside of the tin to loosen the cheesecake from it, then leave to cool in the tin. Remove, and serve cold.

Make-Ahead Cheesecake

Serves 4–6

Base
6 trifle sponges
Filling
500 g (1 lb) low-fat soft cheese
60 g (2 oz) butter
½ teaspoon vanilla essence
1 tablespoon cornflour
2 tablespoons top of the milk
2 eggs, separated
60 g (2 oz) castor sugar

Line the base and grease the inside of an 18 cm (7 inch) loose-based square cake tin. Cut the trifle sponges in horizontal slices thin enough to cover the base of the tin. Lay them in the tin.

Mash the cheese with a fork to soften it. Melt the butter without letting it get hot, and mix it into the cheese smoothly with the vanilla essence. Blend the cornflour with the milk until smooth, and stir into the cheese mixture. Mix in the egg yolks and beat well until the mixture is light. Whisk the egg whites until fairly stiff and glossy, gradually whisking in the sugar. Fold the egg whites into the cheese mixture. Turn the mixture gently into the tin, and level the surface with a palette knife. Heat the oven to 230°C, 450°F, Gas 8, and put the tin in the very hot oven. Reduce the heat at once to 180°C, 350°F, Gas 4, and bake for 25–35 minutes or until the cheesecake is just firm in the centre. Cool in the turned-off oven for 10 minutes. Remove from the oven and finish cooling in the tin. Then cover loosely with foil and refrigerate for 12–18 hours until wanted for use.

Grapefruit Cheesecake Bars

Serves 8

Base
90 g (3 oz) butter
175 g (6 oz) digestive biscuit crumbs
1 teaspoon grated lemon rind
Filling
250 g (8 oz) full-fat soft cheese
1 teaspoon grated lemon rind
2 grapefruits
1×397 g (14 oz) can sweetened
    condensed milk
3–4 tablespoons lemon juice

Cut a piece of bakewell paper which will fit the base of an 18×28 cm (7×11 inch) baking tin at least 4 cm (1½ inches) deep and overhang on opposite sides. Line the tin with it. Grease the uncovered sides lightly. Melt the butter and work in the crumbs and lemon rind. Press the mixture evenly all over the base of the tin. Chill while making the filling.

Beat the cheese until soft, adding the lemon rind. Remove all skin, pith and pips from the grapefruits over a soup plate, to catch any juice. Chop the flesh into small bits, and keep aside. Little by little, beat the condensed milk, grapefruit juice and lemon juice into the cheese (use only 3 tablespoons lemon juice if the grapefruits are very juicy). Fold in the bits of fruit. Turn the mixture on to the chilled base, and chill again for 4 hours or until firmly set. Cut into bars for serving.

NOTE: for easy cutting, remove the cheesecake from the tin first, by lifting the two overhanging edges of bakewell paper.

Simple Milk Cheesecake

Serves 4

Base
175 g (6 oz) shortcrust pastry
Filling
175 g (6 oz) home-made milk curd cheese,
    slightly salted (see page 11), or
    low-fat soft cheese
30 g (1 oz) butter
grated rind ½ lemon
30 g (1 oz) castor sugar
1 tablespoon flour
salt
1 egg
100 ml (4 fl oz) milk

Line the base and grease the inside of an 18 cm (7 inch) flan ring on a baking sheet. Roll out the pastry on a lightly floured board and use to line the ring. Chill while making the filling.

Sieve the cheese. Melt the butter without letting it get hot and beat it into the cheese with the lemon rind. Mix and beat in the sugar, flour and a pinch of salt. Beat the egg lightly, and add it with the milk. Mix well, leaving no lumps. Pour the mixture into the chilled pastry case, and bake at 190°C, 375°F, Gas 5, for 45 minutes or until just firm and light golllden-brown. Remove the flan ring and serve, warm or cold, with cream and golden syrup.

Low-Fat Peach or Mandarin Cheesecake
Serves 6

Base
2–3 tablespoons redcurrant jelly
4 teaspoons rum or sweet sherry
125 g (4 oz) wheat crispbread crumbs

Filling and Topping
1×312 g (11 oz) can peaches or mandarin
    oranges in syrup
grated rind and juice 1 lemon
2 packets (30 g/1 oz) gelatine
3 eggs, separated
250 g (8 oz) castor sugar
1×226 g (8 oz) carton cottage cheese
150 ml ($\frac{1}{4}$ pint) natural yogurt
salt
glacé cherries to decorate

Line a 20 cm (8 inch) loose-based shallow cake tin with bakewell paper. Warm the redcurrant jelly gently until it melts. Mix in the rum or sherry, then mix the liquid with the crumbs. Press the mixture evenly all over the base of the tin. Chill.

Drain the fruit over a bowl reserving the syrup. Finely chop all except 5 pieces and keep both chopped and whole fruit aside. Strain the lemon juice into a heatproof measuring jug and make the liquid quantity up to 150 ml ($\frac{1}{4}$ pint) with reserved syrup. Sprinkle on the gelatine and leave for 3–4 minutes to soften. Then stand the jug in a pan of very hot water and stir until the gelatine dissolves. Cool to tepid.

Beat the egg yolks with 150 g (5 oz) of the sugar until thick and pale. Sieve the cheese and beat it in with the yogurt and lemon rind. Whisk the egg whites with a pinch of salt in a separate bowl until stiff, adding the remaining sugar slowly while whisking.

Trickle the dissolved gelatine into the cheese mixture slowly, beating to blend it in thoroughly. Stir in the chopped fruit. Quickly, stir in 1–2 tablespoons egg white, then fold in the rest. Turn the mixture gently on to the chilled base, and leave in a cool place to set. Remove from the tin, peel off the lining paper carefully. Before serving halve the cherries; decorate the top of the cheesecake with the reserved whole fruit and cherries.

Do not freeze this cheesecake.

Summer Dahlia Cheesecake
Serves 4–6

Base
40 g (1$\frac{1}{2}$ oz) margarine
2 teaspoons ginger syrup from jar of
    preserved stem ginger
125 g (4 oz) digestive biscuit crumbs

Filling and Topping
4 tablespoons ginger syrup from jar of
    preserved stem ginger
4 tablespoons cold water
2 packets (30 g/1 oz) gelatine
250 ml (8 fl oz) milk
1 large orange
2 pieces preserved stem ginger
250 g (8 oz) full-fat soft cheese
2 eggs, separated
30 g (1 oz) castor sugar
angelica strips

Line and grease the base of a 15 cm (6 inch) loose-based cake tin. Melt the margarine and syrup, and mix in the crumbs. Press the mixture evenly all over the base of the tin. Chill while making the filling.

Mix 3 tablespoons ginger syrup and the water in a small heatproof bowl. Sprinkle on the gelatine and allow to soften. Then stand the bowl in a pan of very hot water and stir until the gelatine dissolves. Stir in 2 tablespoons milk, and cool to tepid. While cooling, pare off the thin yellow rind of the orange in long strips, and cut into neat long slivers. Drop the orange slivers into boiling water for 2 seconds. Drain. Mix the slivers with the remaining tablespoon ginger syrup and put aside. Remove all white pith from the orange, cut into neat segments without skin or pips, and put aside. Chop the ginger finely, and put a few bits aside for the topping.

Beat the cheese, egg yolks and sugar in a mixing bowl until very soft and creamy. Gradually, beat in the tepid gelatine mixture, remaining milk and chopped ginger. Beat hard until completely blended. Whisk the egg whites until they hold soft peaks, and fold them in. Turn the mixture gently on to the chilled base, and chill again until set. While chilling, drain the orange rind slivers.

To decorate the cheesecake, remove it from the tin. Put the bits of chopped ginger in the centre. Arrange the orange segments and rind slivers round them like the petals of a flower, with the angelica strips, cut into leaves, between them.

Haarlem Cheesecake
Serves 6–8

Base
- 75 g (2½ oz) butter
- 75 g (2½ oz) castor sugar
- 1 egg yolk
- 1 tablespoon milk
- 100 g (3½ oz) self-raising flour
- 1 teaspoon baking powder

Filling
- 600 g (1¼ lb) full-fat soft cheese
- 200 g (7 oz) castor sugar
- juice ½ lemon
- 2 egg yolks
- 30 g (1 oz) cornflour
- 1 teaspoon baking powder
- 3 egg whites

Line the base and grease the inside of a 23 cm (9 inch) loose-based cake tin. Cream the butter and sugar together until soft and light. Whisk the egg yolk with the milk until liquid and fully blended. Combine the liquid with the butter-sugar mixture, then sift and stir in the flour and baking powder together. Spread the base mixture with a knife over the base and 5 cm (2 inches) of the sides of the tin.

For the filling, mash the cheese with a fork if stiff. Beat in the sugar, then the lemon juice and egg yolks. Stir in the cornflour and baking powder together. Beat the egg whites until fairly stiff, and fold into the creamy cheese mixture. Turn gently into the tin, and bake at 180°C, 350°F, Gas 4, for 55 minutes–1 hour or until just set; cover loosely with greaseproof paper if the surface begins to over-brown during cooking. Cool in the turned-off oven. When completely cooled, run a sharp knife round the inside of the tin to loosen the cheesecake. Then remove the tin and serve.

Milk Curd Almond Cheesecake
Serves 4–6

Base
- 40 g (1½ oz) butter
- 60 g (2 oz) digestive biscuit crumbs
- 2 teaspoons castor sugar

Filling
- 125 g (4 oz) home-made milk curd cheese (see page 11)
- 60 g (2 oz) butter
- grated rind and juice ½ lemon
- 1 teaspoon orange juice
- 2 eggs, separated
- 30 g (1 oz) ground almonds
- 30 g (1 oz) semolina
- 60 g (2 oz) castor sugar
- 2–3 drops almond essence
- 2 tablespoons self-raising flour

Topping
- apricot glaze (see page 93)
- toasted flaked almonds (see page 94)

This cheesecake is prepared and baked upside down and inverted just before serving.

Line the base and grease the inside of a 19 cm (7½ inch) sandwich cake tin. Make the base mixture first. Melt the butter and allow it to cool. Then combine it with the crumbs and sugar to make a crumbly mixture. Put aside while you make the filling. Put the cheese in a bowl and break it up with a fork. Melt the butter without letting it get hot. Strain the lemon and orange juice together. Stir the butter, lemon rind, juices and egg yolks into the cheese, then the almonds, semolina, sugar and almond essence. Beat the mixture until well blended. Sift the flour and fold into the mixture. Whisk the egg whites until stiff but not dry, and fold in lightly. Turn the mixture into the prepared tin.

Scatter the crumb mixture lightly and evenly over the cheesecake. Bake at 220°C, 425°F, Gas 7, for 10 minutes, then reduce the heat to 180°C, 350°F, Gas 4, and bake for another 20 minutes or until the cheesecake is firm and dry in the centre when pierced with a thin skewer. Cover loosely with greaseproof paper for the last 10 minutes.

Loosen the cheesecake from the sides of the tin with a flexible spatula or palette knife, then leave to cool in the tin. Invert gently on to a serving plate so that the crumb base is underneath. Peel off the lining paper. Paint the top with the glaze, scatter on the nuts, and serve.

Small cheesecakes

Rice Cheesecakes

Makes 8 small cheesecakes

Cases
  250 g (8 oz) puff pastry
Filling
  60 g (2 oz) long grain rice
  300 ml ($\frac{1}{2}$ pint) milk
  60 g (2 oz) butter
  1 tablespoon castor sugar
  2 eggs
  grated rind $\frac{1}{2}$ lemon
  $\frac{1}{2}$ teaspoon ground mace
  30 g (1 oz) currants

Oil 8×7 cm ($2\frac{3}{4}$ inch) bun tins 3 cm ($1\frac{1}{4}$ inches) deep. Roll out the pastry on a lightly floured board and use to line the tins. Keep the trimmings aside. Prick the bases well. Chill the cases while preparing the filling.

Cook the rice in the milk until very tender; the milk should all be absorbed. Meanwhile soften the butter. Sieve the rice, or purée in an electric blender until smooth. Put the still-warm purée in a mixing bowl, and stir in the butter and sugar. Separate 1 egg, and add the whole egg and egg yolk to the mixture with the lemon rind. Whisk with a fork until fully blended, then stir in the mace and currants. Three-quarters fill the pastry cases with the mixture. Cut narrow strips from the pastry trimmings, and make a lattice pattern or other decorations on the cheesecakes. Brush the cheesecakes with the remaining egg white. Bake at 200°C, 400°F, Gas 6, for 20 minutes or until the cheesecakes are puffed and browned. Reduce the heat to 150°C, 300°F, Gas 2, and bake for another 5 minutes. Loosen the cheesecakes with a knife point and cool in the tins. Serve warm or cold.

Little Curd Cheesecakes

Makes 10–12 small cheesecakes

Cases
  350 g (12 oz) shortcrust pastry
Filling
  250 g (8 oz) thick skimmed milk yogurt
    curd cheese (see recipe below)
  2 eggs
  60 g (2 oz) castor sugar
  grated orange rind
  ground cinnamon, grated nutmeg
  90 g (3 oz) currants and chopped mixed peel,
    mixed

Make the yogurt curd the day before you need it as follows. Mix 90 g (3 oz) dried skimmed milk powder with 600 ml (1 pint) water gradually, without letting lumps form. Warm the mixture to blood heat only. Stir in 2 tablespoons natural low-fat yogurt. Pour into a wide-necked thermos flask and leave for 4–6 hours until a curd forms. Tip out gently into a thin scalded cloth laid in a sieve, and placed over a basin. Leave to drain for 6–8 hours until solid.

Grease the insides of 12×7 cm ($2\frac{3}{4}$ inch) bun tins 3 cm ($1\frac{1}{4}$ inches) deep. Roll out the pastry on a lightly floured board and use to line the tins. Chill while making the filling.

Beat the eggs until frothy. Then gradually beat in the sugar. When the mixture is pale, thick and light, beat in the cheese little by little, incorporating each addition thoroughly until very smooth. Sprinkle a good pinch of orange rind and a pinch each of cinnamon and nutmeg on the dried fruit, and stir into the mixture. Fill the pastry cases not more than two-thirds full each. Bake at 180°C, 350°F, Gas 4, for 20–30 minutes until light gold. Cool for 10 minutes in the tins to firm up the cheesecakes, then finish cooling on a wire rack. Serve warm or cold.

Hot Cheesecake Pastries
Serves 6

Pastry Rounds
300–325 g (10–11 oz) shortcrust or rich
   shortcrust pastry (see page 14)
Filling
2×85 g (3 oz) packets Philadelphia soft cheese
1½ teaspoons lemon juice, or to taste
½ tablespoon grated lemon rind
30 g (1 oz) castor sugar, or to taste
Topping
toasted flaked almonds (see page 94)
Melba sauce (see page 92)

Roll out the pastry on a lightly floured board and cut out 18×7.5 cm (3 inch) rounds. Bake on greased baking sheets at 220°C, 425°F, Gas 7, for 6–8 minutes until lightly browned. Cool while making the filling.

Bring the cheese up to room temperature. Put all the filling ingredients in a mixing bowl and beat together until blended. Taste the filling and add extra lemon juice or sweetening if desired. Put 3 pastry rounds together with 1 tablespoon filling spread between each. Add a small dab of filling on the top round and sprinkle with nuts. Continue until you have 6 pastries and then bake at 200°C, 400°F, Gas 6, for 7–9 minutes. Serve as a hot dessert, with Melba sauce.

Leicester Cheesecakes
Makes 12 small cheesecakes

Cases
350 g (12 oz) puff pastry
Filling
125 g (4 oz) home-made milk
   curd cheese (see page 11)
   or low-fat soft cheese
60 g (2 oz) soft tub margarine
60 g (2 oz) castor sugar
60 g (2 oz) fine dry white breadcrumbs
1 egg
1 egg yolk
175 g (6 oz) mixed currants and sultanas
1 tablespoon single cream
grated nutmeg
½ teaspoon grated lemon rind
2 teaspoons light rum

Grease the insides of 12×7 cm (2¾ inch) bun tins 3 cm (1¼ inches) deep. Roll out the pastry on a lightly floured board and use to line the tins. Prick the bottoms well. Chill while preparing the filling.

Beat the cheese with the margarine until smooth and softened. Mix in the sugar and breadcrumbs. Beat together the whole egg and egg yolk and mix into the cheese with the fruit, cream, a pinch of nutmeg, the lemon rind and rum. The mixture will be fairly wet. Divide it between the pastry cases. Bake at 220°C, 425°F, Gas 7, for 15 minutes, then reduce the heat to 170°C, 325°F, Gas 3, and bake for another 10–15 minutes or until the cheesecakes are firm in the centre. Cool on a wire rack. Eat warm or cold.

Welsh Cheesecakes
Makes 16 small cheesecakes

Cases
150 g (5 oz) shortcrust pastry
3–4 tablespoons raspberry jam
Filling
60 g (2 oz) butter
60 g (2 oz) castor sugar
1 egg
90 g (3 oz) self-raising flour
grated rind ½ lemon
milk as required
Topping
icing sugar

Grease the insides of 16 shallow tartlet tins. Roll out the pastry on a lightly floured board and use to line the tins. Put ½ teaspoon jam in the bottom of each. Decorate the edges as desired. Chill while making the filling.

Soften the butter and beat it together with the sugar until light and fluffy. Beat the egg until liquid, then beat it into the butter-sugar mixture alternately with the flour. Beat in the lemon rind, and enough milk to make the mixture a soft dropping consistency. Divide the mixture into the chilled cases. Bake at 190°C, 375°F, Gas 5, for 15–20 minutes or until the tartlets are firm and light gold. Cool on a wire rack. When cold, dust the tops with icing sugar.

Little Crumb Cheesecakes
Makes 9–10 small cheesecakes

250 g (8 oz) unsalted curd
    cheese (see note below)
    or cottage cheese
30 g (1 oz) soft white breadcrumbs
30 g (1 oz) sugar
$\frac{1}{4}$ teaspoon each grated nutmeg,
    ground cloves and allspice
$\frac{1}{2}$ teaspoon salt
3 eggs
4 teaspoons butter

If using cottage cheese make sure it is well drained. Spread the cheese all over a shallow plate and leave in the refrigerator, uncovered, to dry out overnight.

Grease the insides of 10×7 cm ($2\frac{3}{4}$ inch) bun tins 3 cm ($1\frac{1}{4}$ inches) deep. Sieve the cheese, then beat in all the other ingredients (except the butter) in the order given, adding the eggs one at a time. Beat until smooth. Alternatively, put the eggs first, then the other ingredients, into the goblet of an electric blender and blend on medium speed until smooth.

Put the cheesecake mixture into the tins, filling them only about three-quarters full. Bake for 20–25 minutes at 190°C, 375°F, Gas 5, until firm. Just before the end of the cooking time melt the butter. Sprinkle over the cheesecakes and return to the oven for 4–5 minutes. Cool in the tins.

These very light little cheesecakes are better eaten while still just warm.

NOTE: unsalted curd cheese is obtainable from health food shops if you do not make your own.

Lemon Cream Cheesecakes
Makes 18 small cheesecakes

Cases
    175 g (6 oz) puff pastry
Filling
    90 g (3 oz) butter
    3 boudoir or sponge finger biscuits
    grated rind $1\frac{1}{2}$ small lemons
    40 g ($1\frac{1}{2}$ oz) icing sugar, or to taste
    ground cinnamon, grated nutmeg
    juice 1 lemon
    60 g (2 oz) low-fat soft cheese
    3 tablespoons single cream
    1 egg
    1 egg yolk

Grease the insides of 18 shallow tartlet tins. Roll out the pastry on a lightly floured board and use to line the tins. Chill while making the filling.

Soften the butter. Crush the biscuits to fine even crumbs. Mix in the lemon rind, then work in the butter, icing sugar and a pinch each of cinnamon and nutmeg. Mix in the lemon juice. Separately, beat the cheese until soft, blend in the cream, then mix in the egg and egg yolk. Combine the cheese mixture little by little with the lemon-butter mixture, blending thoroughly until smooth. (Alternatively, put all the filling ingredients—liquids first, then crumbs and rind—in the goblet of an electric blender, and process at medium speed until smooth.)

Divide the mixture between the chilled pastry cases. Bake at 190°C, 375°F, Gas 5, for 20 minutes or until just firm and golden. Cool in the turned-off oven with the door ajar. Serve cold.

Top: Queen Anne Boleyn's Cheesecakes; bottom: Mrs Beeton's Lemon Cheesecakes, 1861

Mrs Beeton's Lemon Cheesecakes, 1861

Makes 24 small cheesecakes

Cases
750 g (1½ lb) puff pastry
Filling
60 g (2 oz) butter
250 g (8 oz) sugar
grated rind 1 lemon
juice 1½ lemons
3 eggs
4 oz Marie biscuit crumbs

Make the lemon curd filling days or even 2–3 weeks ahead. Put the butter, sugar and lemon rind in a saucepan. Strain in the lemon juice, then mix in the eggs thoroughly with a fork. Stir over very gentle heat until the sugar dissolves, and continue stirring until the mixture is the colour and consistency of honey. Turn into heated, wide-necked glass jars and cover loosely with waxed paper discs. When cold, press the discs flat on the surface of the curd, cover the jars tightly, and refrigerate until needed. The mixture will keep for several weeks.

To make the cheesecakes, roll out the pastry thinly on a lightly floured board and chill for 15 minutes. Grease the insides of 24×7 cm (2¾ inch) bun tins 3 cm (1¼ inches) deep, and line with the pastry. Mix the crumbs thoroughly with the lemon curd mixture. Fill the cases two-thirds full with the mixture. Bake at 200°C, 400°F, Gas 6, for 12–14 minutes until well risen and browned. Cool on a wire rack. Serve warm or cold.

Queen Anne Boleyn's Cheesecakes

Makes 10 small cheesecakes

Cases
300 g (10 oz) puff pastry
Filling
1 egg
3 egg yolks
salt
600 ml (1 pint) milk
1½ teaspoons butter
80 ml (3 fl oz) whipping cream
castor sugar as required
2 teaspoons sweet sherry
1 teaspoon rosewater (optional)
15 g (½ oz) currants
ground cinnamon

Grease the insides of 10×7 cm (2¾ inch) bun tins 3 cm (1¼ inches) deep. Roll out the pastry on a lightly floured board and use to line the tins. Chill while making the filling.

In a saucepan, beat the egg and egg yolks until liquid, with a few grains of salt. Mix in the milk. Heat gently, stirring continuously, until the mixture comes to the boil and curdles. Lay a thin cloth in a sieve and turn in the curds. Leave to drain and cool for 30 minutes–1 hour, then transfer to a bowl. Cream the butter until very soft and stir it into the curds. Whip the cream and sweeten with sugar. Then stir in the cream with the sherry and the rosewater if used. Add the currants and a good pinch of cinnamon. Three-quarters fill the pastry cases, and bake at 220°C, 425°F, Gas 7, for 20–25 minutes, or until firm and lightly browned. Cool on a wire rack. Serve warm or cold.

Mandarin Cheesecakes

Makes 20 small cheesecakes

Cases
150 g (5 oz) hard block margarine
2 tablespoons cold water
250 g (8 oz) flour
Filling
250 g (8 oz) full-fat soft cheese
60 g (2 oz) castor sugar
3 tablespoons single cream
Topping
1×298 g (11 oz) can mandarin oranges
apricot glaze (see page 93)

Grease the insides of 20 shallow tartlet tins. Soften the margarine and cream it with the water and with 90 g (3 oz) of the flour until well blended. Gradually work in the remaining flour, to make a smooth dough. Knead until free of cracks. Roll out on a lightly floured board, and use to line the tins. Put a greased circle of greaseproof paper inside each pastry case, fill with dried beans or rice, and bake blind at 200°C, 400°F, Gas 6, for 20 minutes. Cool.

Beat the cheese until soft and creamy, then beat in the sugar and cream to make a smooth, fully-blended mixture. Divide the mixture into the cooled, baked pastry cases. Drain the can of mandarin oranges very thoroughly. Arrange the fruit on the tartlets decoratively, and brush lightly with warm glaze.

Individual Orange Cheesecakes
Serves 2

Bases
  2 digestive biscuits
Filling
  2 heaped tablespoons dried skimmed
    milk powder
  150 ml ($\frac{1}{4}$ pint) cold water
  1 egg, separated
  1 tablespoon castor sugar
  3 tablespoons orange juice
  1$\frac{1}{2}$ teaspoons gelatine
  1×113 g (4 oz) carton cottage cheese
  salt
Topping
  $\frac{1}{4}$ teaspoon ground cinnamon
  $\frac{1}{4}$ teaspoon castor sugar

Put the biscuits into 2×7.5 cm (3 inch) straight-sided ramekins. In a small saucepan, mix the skimmed milk powder with enough water to make a smooth paste, then gradually mix in the rest of the water. Beat the egg yolk lightly, then stir it into the milk mixture with the sugar. Heat very gently, stirring all over the base of the pan, until the custard thickens. Cover, and leave aside to cool to tepid.

Put the orange juice in a small heatproof bowl, sprinkle on the gelatine and allow to soften. Then stand the bowl in a pan of very hot water and stir until the gelatine dissolves. Cool to tepid. Sieve the cheese into the cooled custard, mix in until fully blended, then gradually trickle in the gelatine mixture, stirring well to prevent lumps forming. Whisk the egg white with a pinch of salt until stiff but not dry, and fold into the cheese custard. Spoon half the mixture gently into each ramekin and leave to set. Before serving, mix the cinnamon and sugar and sprinkle over the top of the mixture.

To vary:

Orange and Chocolate Cheesecakes

Make as above but use chocolate digestive biscuits (chocolate side up), and sprinkle with grated chocolate instead of cinnamon and sugar.

Little Summer Orange Cheesecakes
Makes 18 small cheesecakes

Cases
  175 g (6 oz) puff pastry
Filling
  90 g (3 oz) butter
  3 boudoir or sponge finger biscuits
  grated rind $\frac{1}{2}$ large orange
  30 g (1 oz) icing sugar, or to taste
  ground cinnamon
  juice $\frac{1}{2}$ large orange
  lemon juice as required
  3 tablespoons single cream
  60 g (2 oz) low-fat soft cheese
  1 large egg

Grease the insides of 18 shallow tartlet tins. Roll out the pastry on a lightly floured board and use to line the tins. Chill while making the filling.

Soften the butter. Crush the biscuits to fine even crumbs. Mix in the grated rind, then work in the butter, icing sugar and a small pinch of cinnamon. Mix in the orange and lemon juice slowly. Separately, blend the cream with the cheese, and beat until very soft. Then beat in the egg. Combine the cheese mixture with the butter-orange mixture little by little, beating until smooth. (Alternatively, put all the filling ingredients—liquids first, crumbs last—in the goblet of an electric blender and process on medium speed until smooth.)

Divide the mixture into the chilled pastry cases. Bake at 190°C, 375°F, Gas 5, for 20 minutes. Cool in the turned-off oven with the door ajar.

Ground Rice Cheesecakes

Makes 12 small cheesecakes

Cases
350 g (12 oz) puff pastry
Filling
60 g (2 oz) butter
60 g (2 oz) castor sugar
60 g (2 oz) ground rice
ground cinnamon
1 tablespoon currants
1 egg

Grease the insides of 12×7 cm (2¾ inch) bun tins 3 cm (1¼ inches) deep. Roll out the pastry on a lightly floured board and use to line the tins. Chill while making the filling.

Soften the butter. Cream the butter and sugar together until thick and pale. Mix in the ground rice, blending until smooth. Mix in a good pinch of cinnamon and the currants. Beat the egg lightly until liquid, then blend into the butter-sugar mixture. Divide the mixture between the chilled cases. Bake at 190°C, 375°F, Gas 5, for about 20 minutes until well risen and lightly coloured. Cool in the turned-off oven with the door ajar. Eat within 48 hours.

Mrs Raffald's Curd Cheesecakes, 1782

Makes 12 small cheesecakes

250 g (8 oz) home-made milk curd cheese (see page 11)
60 g (2 oz) butter
175 g (6 oz) soft white breadcrumbs
½ teaspoon grated nutmeg
1 teaspoon grated lemon rind
1 tablespoon white wine
30 g (1 oz) castor sugar

Grease 12×7 cm (2¾ inch) bun tins 3 cm (1¼ inches) deep. Rub the cheese and butter together through a sieve into a clean, dry bowl. Make sure the breadcrumbs are loose, fine and even. Stir them into the mixture. Scatter in the nutmeg and lemon rind, sprinkle on the wine and add the sugar. Mix well. Fill the bun tins two-thirds full with the mixture. Bake at 180°C, 350°F, Gas 4, for 25–30 minutes until firm and golden-brown. Cool in the tins. These cheesecakes are best eaten while still just warm.

Rich Almond Cheesecakes

Makes 12–14 small cheesecakes

Cases
400 g (14 oz) puff pastry
Filling
60 g (2 oz) butter
90 g (3 oz) ground almonds
2 tablespoons orange juice
1–2 drops almond essence
60 g (2 oz) icing sugar
grated rind ½ lemon
1 tablespoon flour
2 eggs
3 tablespoons single cream
Topping
toasted flaked almonds (see page 94)

Lightly grease the insides of 14×7 cm (2¾ inch) bun tins 3 cm (1¼ inches) deep. Roll out the pastry on a lightly floured board and use to line the tins. Chill while making the filling.

Soften the butter. Work the ground almonds to a paste with the orange juice and almond essence. Work in the butter until fully blended, adding the icing sugar gradually while doing so. Mix in the lemon rind and flour. Separately, beat the eggs lightly until liquid and mix with the cream. Blend the liquid into the almond mixture, little by little to prevent it separating. Spoon the mixture into the chilled pastry cases, filling them just over half-full. Sprinkle with the nuts. Bake at 190°C, 375°F, Gas 5, for 25 minutes or until risen and lightly browned. Cool in the turned-off oven with the door ajar for 20 minutes, then finish cooling on a wire rack. Eat within 24 hours.

Do not freeze these cheesecakes.

Richmond Cheesecakes

Makes 16–18 small cheesecakes

Cases
560 g (1 lb 2 oz) puff pastry
Filling
90 g (3 oz) butter
1×113 g (4 oz) carton cottage cheese
150 g (5 oz) dryish mashed potato
90 g (3 oz) castor sugar
30 g (1 oz) ground almonds
1 egg
2 tablespoons brandy
1 tablespoon lemon juice
2–3 drops almond essence
grated nutmeg

Grease the insides of 18×7 cm (2¾ inch) bun tins 3 cm (1¼ inches) deep. Roll out the pastry on a lightly floured board and use to line the tins. Chill while preparing the filling.

Soften the butter. Sieve the cheese and blend it thoroughly with the butter. Beat the potato, sugar and ground almonds together until smooth, then mix them into the cheese with a spoon. In a separate bowl, beat the egg and brandy until blended. Stir them into the cheese mixture, then mix in the lemon juice, almond essence and a pinch of nutmeg. Half-fill the pastry cases with the mixture. Bake at 220°C, 425°F, Gas 7, for 8 minutes, then lower the heat to 190°C, 375°F, Gas 5, and bake for another 25 minutes, or until the cheesecakes are just set and lightly browned. Cool in the turned-off oven for 10 minutes, then finish cooling in the tins at room temperature. Serve warm or cold.

Bread-and-Cream Cheesecakes

Makes 12 small cheesecakes

Cases
350 g (12 oz) shortcrust pastry
Filling
175 g (6 oz) sliced white bread
300 ml (½ pint) single cream
125 g (4 oz) butter
½ teaspoon grated nutmeg
4 eggs
125 g (4 oz) currants
2–3 teaspoons brandy

Start making the filling before the cases. Cut the crusts off the bread, tear into bits and put in a basin. Heat the cream to boiling point, and pour over the bread. Leave to stand for 2 hours.

While soaking, grease the insides of 12×7 cm (2¾ inch) bun tins 3 cm (1¼ inches) deep. Roll out the pastry on a lightly floured board and use to line the tins. Chill.

Soften the butter and beat until creamy with the nutmeg. Then beat the flavoured butter into the bread and cream, making a well-blended, fairly smooth mixture. Beat the eggs until liquid, then beat gradually into the cream mixture. Stir in the currants and brandy. Divide the mixture between the cases. Bake at 180°C, 350°F, Gas 4, for about 45 minutes or until firm and light gold. Cool on a wire rack. Serve cold.

Almond Cheesecakes

Makes 24 small cheesecakes

Cases
250 g (8 oz) puff pastry
Filling and Topping
125 g (4 oz) home-made milk curd cheese (see page 11)
90 g (3 oz) butter
2 eggs
¼ teaspoon salt
2 tablespoons brandy
40 g (1½ oz) chopped almonds
30 g (1 oz) castor sugar
flaked almonds to decorate

Grease 24 shallow tartlet tins. Roll out the pastry on a lightly floured board and use to line the tins. Prick the bases well. Chill while preparing the filling.

Mash the cheese with a fork, or rub through a sieve. Melt the butter and beat the eggs until liquid. Beat the butter and eggs into the cheese, then beat in the salt and brandy. Make sure the almonds are finely chopped or coarsely ground. Beat them into the cheese with the sugar. Divide the mixture between the pastry cases and sprinkle a few flaked almonds on top of each cheesecake. Bake at 220°C, 425°F, Gas 7, for 15–20 minutes until the cheesecakes are well risen and browned. Cool on a wire rack. Eat warm or cold.

Sherry and Almond Cheesecakes

Makes 15–16 small cheesecakes

60 g (2 oz) butter
125 g (4 oz) ground almonds
3 egg yolks
2 egg whites
125 g (4 oz) castor sugar
grated rind 1 lemon
grated nutmeg
1 tablespoon sweet sherry

Line with paper cases 16×7 cm (2¾ inch) tartlet or small bun tins. Melt the butter and leave to cool slightly. Beat together in a mixing bowl the almonds, egg yolks and whites, sugar, lemon rind and a good pinch of nutmeg. Stir in the butter with the sherry. Spoon the mixture into the cases, filling only half-full. Bake at 180°C, 350°F, Gas 4, for 25–35 minutes until firm and golden-brown. Cool on a wire rack.

Traditional Small Cheesecakes

Makes 12–14 small cheesecakes

Cases
400 g (14 oz) shortcrust pastry
Filling
125 g (4 oz) butter
3 eggs
300 ml (½ pint) double cream
2 tablespoons brandy
30 g (1 oz) Marie biscuit crumbs
30 g (1 oz) currants

Grease the insides of 14×7 cm (2¾ inch) bun tins 3 cm (1¼ inches) deep. Roll out the pastry on a lightly floured board and use to line the tins. Chill until the filling is prepared.

Melt the butter gently without letting it get hot. Leave to cool to tepid. Beat the eggs into the cream until blended. Mix in the butter and brandy. Slowly mix in the crumbs to prevent them making lumps. Half-fill the pastry cases and put a few currants in each one. Bake at 200°C, 400°F, Gas 6, for 12–15 minutes until well risen and golden-brown. Lower the heat to 170°C, 325°F, Gas 3, and bake for a further 5 minutes. Cool on a wire rack. Serve while freshly baked, preferably while still just warm.

This is a rich recipe by modern standards.

Victorian Curd Cheesecakes

Makes 24 small cheesecakes

Cases
750 g (1½ lb) puff pastry
Filling
60 g (2 oz) macaroons or ratafias
60 g (2 oz) candied peel (optional)
125 g (4 oz) butter
1½ tablespoons egg white
500 g (1 lb) low-fat soft cheese
1 large egg yolk
salt
grated rind ½ small lemon
90 g (3 oz) castor sugar, or to taste
1–2 drops almond essence (if using
    almond macaroons or ratafias)

Grease the insides of 24×7 cm (2¾ inch) bun tins 3 cm (1¼ inches) deep. Roll out the pastry on a lightly floured board and use to line the tins. Chill while making the filling.

Crush the macaroons to fine crumbs, removing any rice paper. Chop the peel. Soften the butter and beat the egg white until liquid. Beat the cheese until soft and creamy, then beat in the butter, egg yolk, egg white, a pinch of salt, the lemon rind, peel, sugar and almond essence. Add the crumbs last and mix thoroughly. Fill the cases not quite full. Bake at 190°C, 375°F, Gas 5, for 25–30 minutes or until risen and lightly browned. Cool for 20 minutes in the turned-off oven with the door ajar, then finish cooling on a wire rack.

Derby Curd Cheesecakes

Makes 14–16 small cheesecakes

Cases

500 g (1 lb) shortcrust pastry

Filling

300 g (10 oz) home-made milk curd cheese
(see page 11), or cottage cheese
2 egg yolks
30 g (1 oz) butter
½ teaspoon grated lemon rind
1 teaspoon grated nutmeg
60 g (2 oz) castor sugar
60 g (2 oz) sponge cake crumbs or
soft white breadcrumbs
40 g (1½ oz) currants

Grease the insides of 16×7 cm (2¾ inch) bun tins 3 cm (1¼ inches) deep. Roll out the pastry on a lightly floured board and use to line the tins. Chill while preparing the filling.

If using cottage cheese, sieve and drain it first. Stir the egg yolks into the cheese until blended. Melt and cool the butter and stir it in, then stir in all the remaining ingredients. Fill the pastry cases two-thirds full with the mixture. Bake for 15–20 minutes at 220°C, 425°F, Gas 7, or until firm and lightly browned. Cool for 10 minutes in the tins, then finish cooling on a wire rack. Eat warm or cold.

Cambridge Cheesecakes

Makes 16 small cheesecakes

Cases

500 g (1 lb) shortcrust pastry

Filling

90 g (3 oz) butter
125 g (4 oz) castor sugar
1 egg yolk
60 g (2 oz) currants
60 g (2 oz) chopped mixed peel
2 tablespoons flour
2 teaspoons light rum
2 egg whites

Grease well the insides of 16×7 cm (2¾ inch) bun tins 3 cm (1¼ inches) deep. Roll out the pastry on a lightly floured board, and use to line the tins. Prick the bases well, and chill while preparing the filling.

Soften the butter and beat together with the sugar until very soft and creamy. Beat in the egg yolk. Toss

the dried fruit in the flour, separating any lumps, and stir into the mixture with the rum. Whisk the egg whites until stiff. Stir 3 tablespoons into the mixture to loosen it, then fold in the rest. Fill the pastry cases three-quarters full. Bake at 220°C, 425°F, Gas 7, for about 15 minutes until well browned. Lift out carefully on to a wire rack; the cheesecakes are fragile while warm, being fatty. Serve just warm, or cool and re-warm for a few minutes before serving.

Folkestone Cheesecakes

Makes 12 small cheesecakes

Cases

350 g (12 oz) shortcrust pastry

Filling

40 g (1½ oz) semolina
300 ml (½ pint) milk
30 g (1 oz) butter
60 g (2 oz) castor sugar
grated rind ¼ lemon
1 egg
salt

Topping

1 tablespoon currants

Grease the insides of 12×7 cm (2¾ inch) bun tins 3 cm (1¼ inches) deep. Roll out the pastry on a lightly floured board and use to line the tins. Put a greased circle of greaseproof paper inside each pastry case, fill with dried beans or rice, and bake blind at 200°C, 400°F, Gas 6, for 6–8 minutes. Remove from the oven, take out the filling and paper, and put aside while making the filling.

Put the semolina and milk in a saucepan, heat, and simmer for 10 minutes. Cut the butter into small pieces, and stir in with the sugar and lemon rind. Beat the egg and stir into the mixture with a pinch of salt. Continue simmering for 3 minutes, stirring continuously. Leave to cool for 5 minutes. Fill the pastry cases three-quarters full with the mixture, and top each cheesecake with a few currants. Bake at 180°C, 350°F, Gas 4, for 30–40 minutes until firm and golden-brown. Cool on a wire rack and serve warm or cold.

Toppings and sauces

Golden Crumb Topping
Covers 2×18 cm (7 inch) cheesecakes

175 g (6 oz) dry white breadcrumbs
90 g (3 oz) butter
60 g (2 oz) castor sugar
1 teaspoon ground cinnamon

Crush the breadcrumbs until very fine and even. Melt the butter in a frying pan, add the crumbs, and stir over gentle heat, turning the crumbs over until they are evenly golden. Stir in the sugar and cinnamon, and turn at once on to a baking sheet or large plate to cool. Store in an airtight jar in the refrigerator for up to 2 weeks. Sprinkle on a plain or glazed cheesecake just before serving.

To vary:

Golden Oatmeal Topping
Covers 2×18 cm (7 inch) cheesecakes

90 g (3 oz) butter
150 g (5 oz) dry white breadcrumbs
30 g (1 oz) coarse oatmeal
60 g (2 oz) sugar
$\frac{1}{2}$ teaspoon ground cinnamon
$\frac{1}{4}$ teaspoon grated nutmeg

Melt the butter in a large frying pan. Stir in the breadcrumbs and oatmeal, and turn them over in the butter until light gold and crisp. Stir in the sugar and spices, scrape together and turn on to a baking sheet. Spread out in an even layer, and cool. Then store in an airtight jar, refrigerated, until needed. The topping keeps for 2–3 weeks. Use instead of biscuit or cake crumbs for sprinkling on strongly lemon-flavoured, tangy or slightly spicy cheesecakes.

Coffee Syrup Sauce
Serves 4

125 g (4 oz) demerara sugar
2 tablespoons cold water
300 ml ($\frac{1}{2}$ pint) strong black coffee
1 teaspoon dark rum

Put the sugar and water in a heavy-based saucepan. Melt the sugar over gentle heat, without stirring. Raise the heat and bring the sugar and water to the boil. Boil fast until the sugar becomes light gold. Quickly stir in the coffee. Stir until the sticky fluid dissolves. Lower the heat, and simmer until the sauce is syrupy. Stir in the rum. Remove from the heat, and allow to cool.

When cold, serve over a coffee, chocolate or rum-flavoured cheesecake.

Chocolate Curls
(for decorating)

Chill a solid block of chocolate until cold and hard. Shave it in long strokes with a vegetable peeler or on the broad slicing blade of a box grater. The shavings will come off as long thin curls. Handle them with care; they are fragile, and should be as long and curly as possible for their best effect.

For broader chocolate curls, or scrolls, break up the chocolate and melt it on a plate over a pan of simmering water. Leave the chocolate to cool on the plate or spread it on an oiled stone or Formica slab until almost set. Scrape off broad curls with a sharp knife held almost horizontally against the chocolate. These broad curls are also called chocolate caraque.

Chill the curls, then pile them lightly on a cheesecake just before serving.

Blackcurrant Purée
(for topping or sauce)
Serves 4–6

1×485 g (1 lb 1½ oz) can or jar
 blackcurrants in syrup
2 teaspoons crème de cassis liqueur (optional)

Drain the fruit and reserve 175 ml (6 fl oz) of the syrup; you will probably need all the syrup from a can or jar. Turn the fruit and syrup into a saucepan, and simmer for 4 minutes. Cool slightly, then process in an electric blender if possible, before sieving; this gives a thicker purée than if the fruit is only sieved. Stir in the liqueur if used, pour into a carton or jug, cover, and chill until required. Reheat gently if desired in a heatproof jug standing in a bain-marie.

To vary:
Other Soft Fruit Purées
Use other soft fruits, alone or mixed, instead of blackcurrants. Blackberries, elderberries, loganberries, raspberries, redcurrants, strawberries or plums all make good purées. Mulberries do not have enough flavour.

If using a liqueur, suit it to the flavour of the fruit. Use crème de cassis with blackberries or elderberries; framboise, kirsch or Cointreau with loganberries, raspberries, redcurrants or strawberries; and mirabelle with plums.

Melba Sauce
Covers 1×15 cm (6 inch) cheesecake or
4 individual helpings

250 g (8 oz) fresh ripe raspberries
2–4 tablespoons white wine, not too dry
3 tablespoons icing sugar, or to taste

Hull and pick over the fruit and spread it on a plate. Sprinkle with 2 tablespoons of the wine and the icing sugar. Leave for 30 minutes, then sieve the fruit and any juice with it into a heatproof bowl. Taste, and add the remaining wine and more icing sugar if you wish. Balance the bowl over a pan of simmering water, and stir for 2 minutes. Cool, then chill before using.

Pineapple Topping
Makes about 80–100 ml (3–4 fl oz)
 (covers 1×23 cm (9 inch) cheesecake)

125 g (4 oz) canned crushed pineapple
 (½ fruit from 1×376 g (13¼ oz) can)
40 g (1½ oz) castor sugar, or to taste
2 tablespoons cold water
1 tablespoon cornflour
½ teaspoon butter
1–2 drops yellow food colouring

Drain the fruit well and process in an electric blender until fairly smooth. Put in a saucepan with the sugar and water. Blend the cornflour to a smooth paste with a little of the mixture, then stir it into the rest of the mixture. Taste and add extra sugar if you wish. Heat very gently, stirring constantly, until the glaze boils and thickens. Stir in the butter and food colouring, and let the butter melt. Pour into a cold container. Spoon over a cheesecake when the topping is almost or quite cold.

Praline Topping
Covers 1×20 cm (8 inch) cheesecake

60 g (2 oz) blanched almonds or hazelnuts
1 teaspoon olive oil
60 g (2 oz) castor sugar
1–2 drops vanilla essence
2 teaspoons boiling water

Chop the nuts. Put the oil in a small frying pan and tilt the pan to film the base with oil. Turn in the nuts and stir constantly over very gentle heat, turning the nuts over, until they are just gilded. Turn them at once on to absorbent kitchen paper.

Oil a stone slab or heavy iron baking sheet. Put the sugar, vanilla essence and water in a small saucepan, preferably one which is white inside. Heat to boiling point, and cook for 4 minutes or until the sugar is just turning gold. Stir in the nuts and turn on to the slab or sheet. Leave until cold and brittle. Break up the brittle and crush it coarsely with a pestle in a mortar, or with a rolling pin; do not grind it in a food mill or blender. Sprinkle over a cheesecake just before serving.

NOTE: make several times the quantity above and store for use in an airtight jar if desired.

Apricot Glaze

Makes about 400 g (14 oz) glaze for storage

500 g (1 lb) apricot jam
2 tablespoons lemon juice
2 tablespoons cold water

Warm the jam slightly, then sieve it into a clean saucepan. Add the other ingredients, and stir over gentle heat until the jam dissolves. Simmer for 4 minutes. While simmering, rinse out a heatproof jar with boiling water. Turn the glaze into the wet jar, cover with a disc of waxed paper and cool. Use a few spoonfuls when tepid and still liquid if needed at once, then cool the rest completely, and cover with an airtight lid or cover like jam. To use stored glaze, reheat by standing the container in very hot water. Cool to tepid before using.

To use, spoon or paint the glaze over the surface of a cheesecake, or over fruit arranged in a decorative pattern on the top.

To vary:
Use the above method for all 4 variations.

Redcurrant Glaze
Use redcurrant jelly instead of apricot jam.
Somerset Glaze
Use apple or crab-apple jelly instead of apricot jam.
Scots Glaze
Use fine shred jelly marmalade (orange or lemon) and 2 teaspoons whisky instead of apricot jam.
Welsh Glaze
Use rowan jelly instead of apricot jam.

Apricot Sauce

Makes about 400 ml ($\frac{3}{4}$ pint) sauce

250 g (8 oz) dried apricots
cold water as required
90 g (3 oz) light soft brown sugar
salt
1 tablespoon orange juice
1–2 teaspoons Cointreau (optional)

Steep the apricots overnight in enough cold water to cover them by 3 cm ($1\frac{1}{4}$ inches). Put both in a saucepan, half-cover and simmer until the fruit is pulpy; add a very little more water if you need to. Sieve or blend both fruit and liquid. Put back in the saucepan, add the sugar and a pinch of salt and stir over gentle heat until the sugar melts. Cool, then add the orange juice and the liqueur if used. Measure and add water to make the sauce up to 400 ml ($\frac{3}{4}$ pint), or to taste. Reheat, or chill to use cold.

Ginger and Apricot Topping or Sauce

Makes about 300 ml ($\frac{1}{2}$ pint) sauce
(covers 1×18 cm (7 inch) cheesecake)

boiling water as required
90 g (3 oz) dried apricots
30 g (1 oz) preserved stem ginger in syrup
100 ml (4 fl oz) whipping cream
2–3 drops lemon juice, or to taste

Pour plenty of boiling water over the apricots and leave overnight. Drain them thoroughly, then sieve or blend them until smooth. Drain the ginger, reserving the syrup, and chop it very finely. Mix with the apricot purée. Whip the cream until it just holds soft peaks, gradually adding 2 tablespoons reserved syrup and 1–2 drops lemon juice. Fold the apricot and ginger mixture into the cream, taste and add extra lemon juice if you wish. Chill before using.

Lemon Sauce

Makes about 400 ml ($\frac{3}{4}$ pint) sauce

rind $\frac{1}{2}$ lemon
300 ml ($\frac{1}{2}$ pint) cold water
90 g (3 oz) castor sugar
80 ml (3 fl oz) lemon juice
2 teaspoons arrowroot
2 drops yellow food colouring
3 tablespoons medium-dry white wine
    or dry sherry (optional)

Pare off the lemon rind in long strips, and steep it in the water, in a saucepan, for 20 minutes. Take it out. Add the sugar to the water, heat to the boil, and simmer, uncovered for 5 minutes. Blend 1 table-spoon of the lemon juice with the arrowroot to make a smooth cream. Remove the pan from the heat, stir in the remaining lemon juice and the food colouring, then stir in the arrowroot cream. Heat again, still stirring, until the sauce thickens and clears. Stir in the wine or sherry if used. Cool, covered, before use.

Fresh Strawberry Topping

Makes about 300 ml ($\frac{1}{2}$ pint)
    (covers 2×23 cm (9 inch) cheesecakes)

250 g (8 oz) fresh strawberries
125 g (4 oz) castor sugar
4 tablespoons cold water
salt
1$\frac{1}{2}$ tablespoons cornflour
1 teaspoon butter

First hull the strawberries, then slice and sieve them, or process in an electric blender. Turn into a small saucepan, and mix in the sugar, water and a few grains of salt. Blend a little of the mixture with the cornflour to make a smooth paste, then combine the paste with the rest of the mixture, taking care not to leave any lumps. Stirring continuously, bring slowly to the boil, and continue stirring until the mixture thickens. Stir in the butter. Skim, and pour into a clean container. Spoon over a cheesecake when the topping has almost completely cooled, or store it in a refrigerator or freezer.

To use from storage first bring to room temperature. Then put in a heatproof bowl over a pan of very hot water, and stir until just liquid.

Toasted Coconut

frying oil
desiccated coconut

Film a large frying pan with just enough oil to cover the base thinly. Put in a layer of coconut not more than 1 cm ($\frac{1}{2}$ inch) thick, and stir rapidly over very gentle heat, turning the coconut over until it is light gold. Do not cease stirring; it burns easily. Turn on to absorbent kitchen paper as soon as it reaches the desired colour. Cool, then store in an airtight jar.

Coconut can also be toasted under the grill, but it is less easy to prevent it burning. Put a layer of coconut on an oiled sheet of foil in the grill pan and grill gently, shaking the pan, until the coconut is lightly toasted. Turn with a spoon, and toast to the colour desired. Cool on absorbent kitchen paper, then store as above.

Use for decorating the sides or top of a cheesecake, or for mixing with biscuit crumbs for a shell or base.

Toasted Flaked Almonds

(for crumb crusts, and for decorating the tops
    and sides of cheesecakes)

1 tablespoon frying oil
125 g (4 oz) flaked almonds

Warm the oil in a large frying pan, tilting the pan to film the base. Tip in the nuts and spread them in as thin a layer as possible. Place over very gentle heat, and turn the nuts over continuously with a metal spatula or spoon until they are golden; do not stop turning them, or they will burn almost instantly. Turn them on to absorbent kitchen paper and pat dry. Leave to cool, then store in a jar with a screwtop lid. The nuts can be crushed to crumbs for covering the sides of a cheesecake.

Index

Adaptable Cheesecake 18
Almond
    Almond and Cinnamon Cheesecake 20
    Almond and Orange Cheesecake 46
    Almond and Sherry Cheese Torte 69
    Almond Cheesecakes 88
    Almond Cheesecakes, Rich 87
    Almond Sponge Cheesecake 19
    Baked Almond Cheesecake 20
    Cheddar and Almond Cheesecake 69
    Milk Curd Almond Cheesecakes 80
    Sherry and Almond Cheesecakes 89
    Toasted Flaked Almonds 94
Alpine Cheesecake 25
Apple
    Apple and Walnut Cheesecake 59
    Apple Glaze 49
    Cheshire and Apple Cheesecake 49
    Soft Lemon and Apple Cheese Flan 74
Apricot
    Apricot Glaze 93
    Apricot Jam Cheesecake 63
    Apricot Sauce 93
    Brandied Apricot Cheesecake 34
    Ginger and Apricot Topping 93
As-You-Like-It Cheesecake 46
Avocado Cheesecake 52

Baked Cheesecakes 17–45
Banana and Chocolate Cheesecake 52
Belgian Cheese Flan, Rich 22
Black Forest Cheesecake 66
Blackcurrant Purée 92
Blackcurrant Skim Cheesecake 53
Bran Flake Dessert Cheesecake 51
Brandied Apricot Cheesecake 35
Bread-and-Cream Cheesecakes 88
Brie Cheesecake, Sweet 28
Buckinghamshire Cherry Cheesecake 74
Budget Cheese Pie 77

Cambridge Cheesecakes 90
Camembert Cheesecake, Savoury 48
Candlelight Cheesecake 19
Cassata Cheesecake 72
Cheddar and Almond Cheesecake 69

Cheddar and Honey Cheese Flan 47
Cheddar Cheesecake 35
Cherry
    Buckinghamshire Cherry Cheesecake 74
    Cherry Charlotte Cheesecake 54
Cheshire and Apple Cheesecake 49
Chiffon Cheesecake 32
Chocolate
    Banana and Chocolate Cheesecake 52
    Chocolate and Lemon Curl Cheesecake 67
    Chocolate Curls 91
    Chocolate Marble Cheesecake 44
    Chocolate Sultana Cheesecake 43
Cider Cheesecake, Rich 48
Cinnamon
    Almond and Cinnamon Cheesecake 20
    Cinnamon Cheesecake with Sour Cream
      Topping 31
    Cinnamon Crumb Cheesecake 42
Coconut-Orange Cheesecake 68
Coconut, Toasted 94
Coffee and Rum Cheesecake 45
Coffee Syrup Sauce 91
Cottage Cheese Torte 17
Cottage Custard Cheesecake 58
Cottage Orange Cheesecake 75
Cottage Supper Cheesecake 75
Creamy Crowd Cheesecake 30
Creamy Pear Cheesecake 70
Creamy Walnut Cheesecake 30
Crumb-Nut Cheesecake 21
Curd and Currant Cheese Flan 76
Currant Cheese Flan, Curd and 76

Derby Curd Cheesecakes 90
Devonshire Cheesecake 51
Dutch Brown Pie 43

Easter Holiday Cheese Gâteau 71

Flan Pastry 14
Folkestone Cheesecakes 90
Freezer Cheesecake 64
French Cheesecake 41
Fridge-Fresh Cheesecake 23

Fruit Cheesecakes 52–57
Fruit Cheesecake, Low-Fat 70
Fruit-Topped Vanilla Cheesecake 38
Fruit Purées 92

Garibaldi Cheesecake 65
Gelatine-Set Cheesecakes 24, 46–67
Ginger and Apricot Topping 93
Ginger and Rum Freezer Cheesecake 64
Ginger and Yogurt Cheesecake 50
Glazes 49, 93
Golden Crumb Topping 91
Golden Oatmeal Topping 91
Grapefruit Cheesecake Bars 78
Grape Cheesecake, White 53
Greek Honey Cheesecake 40
Ground Rice Cheesecake 87
Gruyère Cheesecake, Savoury 47

Haarlem Cheesecake 80
Hereford Curd Cake 23
Highland Cheesecake 58
Hollywood Cheese Flan 68
Honey
    Cheddar and Honey Cheese Flan 47
    Greek Honey Cheesecake 40
    Honey Cheesecake 41
    Three-Cheese Honey Cheesecake 40
Hot Cheesecake Pastries 82

Individual Orange Cheesecakes 86
Italian Cheesecake 26

Lattice Peel Cheesecake 22
Leicester Cheesecakes 82
Lemon
    Chocolate and Lemon Curl Cheesecake 67
    Lemon and Redcurrant Cheesecake 56
    Lemon and Spice Cheesecake 77
    Lemon Cheese Filling 11
    Lemon Cream Cheesecakes 83
    Lemon Flavouring 12
    Lemon Sauce 94
    Mrs. Beeton's Lemon Cheesecakes 84
    One-Stage Lemon Cottage Cheesecake 21
    Soft Lemon Cheesecake 74

Light Cream Cheesecake 31
Lindy's Original Cheesecake 34
Liqueured Party Cheesecake 72
Lime Cheesecake 62
Little Crumb Cheesecakes 83
Little Curd Cheesecakes 81
Little Summer Orange Cheesecakes 86
Loganberry Cheesecake 54
Longley Pineapple Cheesecake 55
Low-Cost Cheesecakes 75–80
Low-Fat Fruit Cheesecake 70
Low-Fat Mandarin Cheesecake 79
Low-Fat Peach Cheesecake 79
Luxemburg Kaes-Kuch 26

Make-Ahead Cheesecake 78
Mandarin Cheesecake, Low-Fat 79
Mandarin Cheesecakes 85
Marmalade Glaze 93
Maryland Party Cheesecake 29
Melba Sauce 92
Meringue-Topped Cheesecake 27
Milk Curd Almond Cheesecakes 80
Milk Curd Cheese 11
Milk Curd Cheesecake 27
Mocha Cheesecake 67
Mrs. Beeton's Lemon Cheesecakes 84

Natural Cheesecake, Rich 33
Nesselrode Cheesecake 63
North Country Curd Tart 76
Nut, Crumb- Cheesecake 21

One-Stage Lemon Cottage Cheesecake 21
Orange
    Almond and Orange Cheesecake 46
    Coconut-Orange Cheesecake 68
    Cottage Orange Cheesecake 75
    Individual Orange Cheesecakes 86
    Little Summer Orange Cheesecakes 86
    Soft Orange Cheese Flan 74
    Summer Orange Cheesecake 60

Party Cheesecakes 63–67
Pashka 73
Peach Cheesecake, Low-Fat 79
Pear Cheesecake, Creamy 70
Pineapple
    Longley Pineapple Cheesecake 55
    Pineapple Cheesecake 39
    Pineapple Jelly Cheesecake 59
    Pineapple Topping 92
Plum Cheesecake 37
Plum Pie Cheesecake 70
Praline Topping 92

Quark Cheesecake, Special 50
Queen Anne Boleyn's Cheesecakes 85

Raspberry Cheesecake, Fresh 57
Redcurrant Cheesecake, Lemon and 56
Redcurrant Glaze 93
Rice Cheesecakes 81
Rice Cheesecakes, Ground 87
Richmond Cheesecakes 88
Rowan Jelly Glaze 93
Rum
    Ginger and Rum Freezer Cheesecake 64
    Coffee and Rum Cheesecake 45
    Rum Lattice Cheesecake 44

Saffron Cheesecake 18
Salzburg Curd Cake 77
Sauces 91–94
Scots Glaze 93
Sherry
    Almond and Sherry Cheese Torte 69
    Sherry and Almond Cheesecakes 89
Shortcrust Pastry, Rich 14
Sicilian Cheese Gâteau 71
Simple Milk Cheesecake 78
Small Cheesecakes 81–99
Snowy Party Cheesecake 17
Soft Lemon Cheesecake 74
Somerset Glaze 93
Soured Cream Cheesecake 34

Soured Cream Topping 31
Spice
    Lemon and Spice Cheesecake 77
    Spice Cheesecake 42
Strawberry Cottage Cheesecake 55
Strawberry-Topped Cheesecake 38
Strawberry Topping, Fresh 94
Sultana
    Chocolate Sultana Cheesecake 43
    Warsaw Sultana Cheesecake 22
Summer Dahlia Cheesecake 79
Summer Orange Cheesecake 60

Tangy Jelly Cheesecake 62
Teatime Fruit Yogurt Cheesecake 39
Ten Minute French Cheesecake 41
Three-Cheese Honey Cheesecake 40
Toasted Coconut 94
Toasted Flaked Almonds 94
Toppings 91–94
Traditional Small Cheesecakes 89
Two-Way Cheesecake 24

Unbaked Cheesecakes 46–74
Upside-Down Cheesecake 23

Vanilla Cheesecake, Fruit-Topped 38
Victorian Curd Cheesecakes 89

Walnut Cheesecake, Apple and 59
Walnut Cheesecake, Creamy 30
Warsaw Sultana Cheesecake 22
Welsh Cheesecakes 82
Welsh Glaze 93
Whipped Cream Cheesecake 66
White Grape Cheesecake 53

Yogurt
    Ginger and Yogurt Cheesecake 50
    Teatime Fruit Yogurt Cheesecake 39
    Yogurt Cheese 11
Yorkshire Cottage Cheesecake 76